52 REAL-LIFE NEGOTIATION CASES

52 REAL-LIFE NEGOTIATION CASES

JON LAVELLE

First published in Great Britain 2015

Blue Ice Publishing Ltd
www.blueiceconsulting.co.uk
Registered UK Company
Registration No. 6436734
VAT Registration: 925 8285 93

In association with
www.negotiation-hub.uk
www.managertoolkits.co.uk

ISBN: 9780955956430

Printed and bound in the UK by TJ International Ltd, Padstow, Cornwall

'Come to the edge,' he said.
'We can't, we're afraid!'
'Come to the edge,' he said.
'We can't, we will fall!'
'Come to the edge,' he said.
And so they came.
And he pushed them.
And they flew.

Guillaume Apollinaire

Jon Lavelle

- Experienced master trainer and workshop facilitator.
- Negotiated personally, and trained negotiators in 26 countries.
- Wide range of well-known corporate clients in technology, pharmaceuticals, finance, engineering, petrochemicals, consumer and retail industries.
- Four times published author.

Jon Lavelle is a pragmatist. Whilst theories play their part, Jon has discovered in his many years of negotiating, and in helping others to achieve great deals, that there's nothing more interesting than real life.

Having worked with thousands of negotiators, from both sales and procurement perspectives, and of course having engaged in countless negotiations himself, Jon has built up a collection of real-life negotiation situations – ones that really happened – from which important insights and lessons can be learned.

With an MBA from Warwick Business School underpinning real-life experience, Jon is well placed to help others to negotiate the best deals they can, whether they're multimillion dollar contracts or just trying to get a discount on a restaurant bill. No matter the size or context of the deal, the strategies, principles and tactics of negotiation are exactly the same.

Jon is also the creator of a series of management toolkits, including the 'Professional Negotiator's Toolkit', 'Advanced Negotiation Toolkit' and the 'Professional Sales & Business Development Toolkit'. For more information visit:

www.managertoolkits.co.uk and www.negotiation-hub.uk

CONTENTS

INTRODUCTION   XI

PART ONE: THE CASES   1

1 LOGIC VS. EMOTION   5

2 CONTROLLING THE NEGOTIATION ENVIRONMENT   11

3 SCARCITY   17

4 INTERESTS VS. POSITIONS   23

5 FROM 'LOSE-LOSE' TO 'WIN-WIN'   29

6 BOILING FROG   35

7 THE POWER OF SILENCE   41

8 THREAT OF SUBSTITUTION   47

9 USING THREAT   53

10 QUOD ERAT DEMONSTRANDUM (QED)   59

11 COGNITIVE DISSONANCE   63

12 BRINKMANSHIP   69

13 PERSONAL AGENDAS   75

14 FATALISM VS. DETERMINISM   81

15 POWER OF LANGUAGE   87

16 EXPLICIT VS. IMPLICIT COMMUNICATION   91

17 GOOD, CHEAP, FAST   99

18 BREAKING DEADLOCKED NEGOTIATIONS   105

19 ONUS TRANSFER   111

20 BATNA AND WALK-AWAY POWER   117

21 'LOSE-LOSE' IS PERFECTLY POSSIBLE   123

22 'WIN-WIN' COLLABORATION   129

23 GETTING THINGS INTO PERSPECTIVE   135

24 REDEFINE THE MARKET   139

25 GO EASY ON THE PEOPLE   143

26 PEOPLE LIE   147

27 RECIPROCITY   151

28 HOLDING YOUR GROUND   157

29 TOO EXPENSIVE   163

30 DON'T DROP YOUR GUARD   167

31 DON'T ASSUME TOO SOON   171

32 POWER PLAY   177

33 BLUFF   183

34 GUILT TRIP   191

35 FUNNY MONEY   195

36 HIGHER AUTHORITY   199

37 GOOD COP, BAD COP   205

38 LAYING DOWN A MARKER   211

39 LIM STRATEGY   217

40 CREATIVITY CREATES A BREAKTHROUGH   221

41 BLOODY MINDEDNESS   227

42 NEGOTIATING FROM ROCK BOTTOM   233

43 LOYALTY OVER TRUTH   239

44 VALUE DISCOVERY   245

45 POWERLESS TO NEGOTIATE   251

46 ZOPA   257

47 YOU'LL HAVE TO DO BETTER   263

48 CORRUPTION AND BRIBERY   269

49 RED HERRING   275

50 WHEN IN ROME – OR ATHENS   281

51 HOSTAGE   285

52 RUSSIAN FRONT   291

PART TWO: DEFINITIONS AND EXPLANATION OF TERMS   **295**

FINAL THOUGHTS...   **341**

INTRODUCTION

How much better do you have to be?

This might sound like a strange question, especially as it's not grounded in a specific context. However, think about it for a moment in relation to you negotiating to agree a deal with a potential customer; a situation in which there are several other potential suppliers in competition with you for the business.

Now, how much better do you have to be in order to win the contract at the expense of the other suppliers?

A horse can win a race by a 'nose'. The winning horse and jockey get all the glory and, whilst in horseracing there are prizes for second and third place, in the commercial negotiation world it is often a case of all or nothing – a case of winner takes all.

So, to come home triumphant or defeated can often hinge on being just a little bit better than the competition. Small improvements or refinements in skill and technique can have a massively disproportionate impact – positively or negatively.

Imagine if you made 52 small improvements – how much better would you then be?

52 CASES

All cases described in this book actually happened in real life. The only editing has been to change some of the details in order to preserve anonymity of people and organisations. For example, all names of people are fictitious, the context may have been adjusted, job titles amended and, in some cases, the industry changed.

It doesn't matter; the sequence of events is the same, as are the insights and lessons.

The cases described span a range of scenarios including business, personal, big, small, successes, failures, triumphs, tragedies, serious, funny, etc.

This is not a 'story' book; it's a learning book. So, whilst most people like stories, the key to getting the most value for you from this book is to think about each case from the perspective of insights and learning. Beyond that you need to ask yourself, 'So, what would I have done in that situation?' or 'What would I do if I were to face a similar situation in my real world?'

Why 52 cases? Originally, there were to be 50 – a nice round number. Then, prior to publication, a couple of other cases warranted inclusion. As the number 52 is associated with a deck of cards, there seemed to be an interesting connection.

Playing cards, playing games, playing your cards right, having a strategy, experimenting with different techniques, having an 'Ace' up your sleeve, playing a 'Joker', using bluff and other tactics, responding with counter-tactics, openly putting all your 'cards' on the table, winning and losing… they're all part of the negotiation 'game'.

Many people enjoy playing card games, and when it's just for fun, many don't mind losing, so long as they have a good game, and hopefully also learn from the process.

The front cover displays the metaphor of chess – another enjoyable game with a strategy, moves, tactics and counter-tactics. Just as each chess piece move can shift the power balance between two parties, and the approach and tactics vary depending with whom you're playing, so it is with negotiation.

Whilst the stakes are a lot higher, and the consequences of losing can be significant in a negative sense, many also enjoy the process of the game we call negotiation.

WHO IS THIS BOOK FOR?

This book has been written for everybody and anybody who needs to negotiate, whether that be in business or their personal life, with external parties and agencies, their internal colleagues, their friends or family.

In order to be the best you can possibly be you need to learn from your own experiences in the real world – from what works for you and what tends not to work.

However, in addition to your personal experiences, this book should accelerate your learning by studying the events and insights of others who have faced equally both triumph and disaster. As Rudyard Kipling said, 'Treat those two imposters just the same.'

One interpretation of treating both triumph and disaster as 'just the same' is that, win or lose, you will still learn something from what happened. If you win, you know what to repeat or do similarly; if you lose, you gain clues about what not to do in the future, or at least that that approach, in that situation, at that time and with that particular party did not work this time around.

The overall goal of this book is to help you to negotiate the very best deals you can – that's it. If you can become proficient in that skill, then your life and results will improve in many ways, in several areas and at multiple levels.

STRUCTURE... WHAT STRUCTURE?

If you're a person who likes structure, then be prepared for a surprise.

Whilst each case is structured in the same way, there is no logical structure to the order in which the cases appear in the book. There are several reasons for this:

1. Lots of negotiation texts are structured according to a chronological process of negotiating, from start to finish. In my experience, and in that of thousands of others, that's not the way negotiations work. Often you meet an impasse, you need to go back in order to go forwards, you need to step sideways and try a different approach, you need to jump a step or even start all over again.

2. Each case is a unique situation and, as such, it is self-contained and more than capable of standing alone.

3. Many of the cases involve tactics and counter-tactics. These do not conform

to a natural 'position' within a negotiation process as most can be used at any point, and so to arrange them in that way would be artificial.

4. Sequencing the cases may constrain your thinking as to when you should or should not use a particular tactic; keep all of the tactics in mind all of the time.

5. Surprise can be a nice thing!

That said, the game of negotiation has its own terminology, and so if when reading the cases in Part One, you come across a term you've not heard before, or for which you want to clarify your understanding, then there's a good chance that this is defined in Part Two.

THANKS

Finally, I would like to thank the countless individuals whom I have met and had the opportunity to work with in a negotiation context over the past 30 years of my professional career. Some have made suggestions for cases for the book, taken from their own real-life experiences.

Many were participants on the negotiation and advanced negotiation skills workshops that I've run around the world. You will see some of these diverse, cultural aspects showing through in some of the cases.

In particular, I would like to thank a number of people with whom I have had the pleasure to work in the joint delivery of negotiation skills programmes, or who have contributed to this subject or book in other ways. In no particular order, Nab Kalsi, Sean Sidney, Ester van Eijck, Jan Jacobs, Steve Blackburn, Tom Hampton, Paulo Vasconcelos, Julian Duckmanton, Andrew Bishop, Judi Hunter, Ian Hunter, Hugh Griffiths, Anil Joshi, Francois Maessen, David Bowman, Andrew Hupert, Hannah Vaughan, Magda Pieta, Antonia Hekkelman-Weld, Richard Summerfield, Jan Valkhof, Mike Jones, Aldo Zoli, LLoyd Wang and the recently (2015), sadly departed James Zhang.

Of course, the risk in producing a list such as this is I inadvertently miss someone off. I hope that's not the case but, if so, and you're reading this, you know where I live, so come round for a couple of drinks on me!

To everyone else... enjoy the cases...

Jon Lavelle

52 REAL-LIFE NEGOTIATION CASES

PART ONE: THE CASES

1 LOGIC VS EMOTION

1 LOGIC VS. EMOTION

Petra's sister, Elaine, is frightened of flying. There is no obvious reason for this; no bad previous experience, just a fear of the plane crashing.

She's not alone; according to the National Institute of Mental Health, 6.5% of people will not board an aircraft for fear of it crashing.

Petra's sister has flown a few times though, when she has had to or there was no other sensible option. However, rather than being a pleasurable experience, these occasions have been filled with fear and dread.

One day Petra spoke to her sister – her house is in Aldershot, England. She tried to persuade her that her fears were unfounded and that she was missing out on some fabulous holidays and other experiences by resisting getting on a plane or booking a foreign holiday. She quoted some statistics about how amazingly safe air travel is, comparing it with death and injury rates for other forms of transport such as driving, getting on a bus or just walking down the street for a pint of milk and a newspaper.

None of this made any difference to her sister's position. So, Petra then resorted to another statistic.

'Elaine, did you know that you have more chance of being kicked to death by a donkey than of dying in an air crash?'

'Petra, my dear,' she replied. *'Did you know, there are very few donkeys in Aldershot?'*

INSIGHTS AND LEARNING

This amusing story demonstrates the importance of emotion and feelings in negotiation, influence, persuasion and action (or inaction). It demonstrates that in some circumstances no amount of logic, statistics, facts or unarguable rationale can persuade a person when there are strong emotional feelings surrounding the situation.

It is often said that even in business, people make decisions at an emotional level and then they seek to justify their decision using logic. For example, have you ever bought anything in your personal life simply because you wanted it, even though under the cold light of rational thought or interrogation it does not entirely make sense?

Impulse purchases are often characterised by high emotional involvement, low cognitive control, and largely reactive behaviour. When your wife comes home from work and sees the new car sitting on the drive (when all you did was to go out to buy a newspaper that morning), you feel reasonably confident, because you have had several hours to think up at least five logical reasons why you needed a new car, today, and why this model is exactly the right one to meet your 'joint' needs!

What makes this behaviour particularly interesting at a psychological level is that once having made an emotionally-fuelled purchase, people not only seek to justify it to others, they also endeavour to justify to themselves why it was the right decision, using logic.

If we all made decisions logically, then most of us would be riding around in very basic, utilitarian cars or riding bicycles – there wouldn't be so many luxury cars on the roads. Women would wear well-made but basic shoes, and only have a few pairs costing maybe $30 each. Men would not wear Rolex or Tag Heuer watches, and couples would order a jug of tap water in the restaurant rather than the £8.00 bottle of Evian.

If you work for an organisation and fly regularly, and if you treat the company's money as though it were your own, you would probably choose the cheapest flight possible, rather than trying to 'explain' to your boss why it is important that you fly with a certain airline, sit in business rather than economy/coach class or stay in a certain hotel.

HOW CAN I USE THIS?

Notwithstanding the importance of emotion, logic is a powerful influence tool that has a huge and legitimate part to play in negotiations. Follow these eight common sense, logical steps to inject objectivity, reason and rationale into your negotiation positions, but do not forget to take into account the emotive and emotional reasons why people might accede or not to your requests.

1. Prepare by working through the situation carefully to ensure that your case is well thought out and supported; examine your assumptions and anticipate the assumptions of the other party and the objections they're likely to raise.

2. Explain why you're making your request or proposing a course of action; giving a rationale for your thinking/proposal is both necessary and powerful.

3. Provide evidence to support your conclusions; charts, graphs, tables, models, statistics and other forms of evidence are compelling; the more formal and backed up by third-party evidence they are, the more persuasive you will be.

4. Use evidence that the other party is not aware of; new information bolsters your credibility, and can give you an 'in-the-moment' advantage as the other

party either needs to react to this new information on the spot, pause and think about it, accept it at face value, withdraw/delay or respond in some other way – 'the ball is in their court'.

5. Relate the current situation to previous ones that were dealt with or resolved using the approach you're recommending; show the other party how this situation is similar by referring to precedent and how that approach proved beneficial.

6. If you sense emotional resistance, empathise and probe for understanding; use unemotional questioning to explore the issues and sources of resistance, then work your way back to irrefutable logic.

7. If the other party defends an irrational position, then use logic to undermine their argument and show its weakness, shortcomings, invalidity or fallibility.

8. If the other party needs more proof from you, then go and find it; by doing so, you're answering their 'objection' and leaving them very little 'wiggle room'.

2 CONTROLLING THE NEGOTIATION ENVIRONMENT

2 CONTROLLING THE NEGOTIATION ENVIRONMENT

In the early 1990's, a Purchasing Manager at a pharmaceutical manufacturing site brought a saw into work one morning.

In his office he had two visitors' chairs with wooden legs.

He proceeded to saw two inches off the back legs of each of the chairs. He then reduced the height of the front legs of each chair but, rather sneakily, cut three inches off these.

Feeling proud of his work, he then observed the people who sat in the chairs, who were usually visiting suppliers, sitting lower down than he (who, incidentally, had a much nicer 'executive' swivel chair with arms and headrest).

Furthermore, he would watch in private amusement as, due to the sneaky additional length taken off the front legs, suppliers found themselves imperceptibly and disconcertingly slipping forward in their seats.

His trick was subtle but effective – enough to unnerve the suppliers without it being so obvious that they were able to expose him for using unprofessional and disruptive tactics.

INSIGHTS AND LEARNING

Whilst this is an amusing story, the author in no way condones such crass behaviour, nor any of the other pathetic, bullying techniques that are used by some negotiators in an attempt to put the other party under pressure, duress or stress. Such tactics include, but are not limited to:

- Keeping the other party waiting in reception way beyond the agreed meeting time.
- Arranging for them to be taken to a meeting room and then left alone without explanation for 20 or 30 minutes.
- Sitting them so they're facing the sun or in the path of a bright angle-poise lamp whilst the other party has their back to the window, thus appearing more as a silhouette whose facial expressions are not easy to read.
- Turning the temperature of the room up above normal.
- Not offering any refreshments.
- Arranging for a telephone to ring during the meeting, taking the call and then saying they need to attend to an urgent matter and asking the visitor to wait.

- Arranging for a knock on the door from a colleague to say that 'Mr/Mrs X from [competing supplier] has arrived'.

The list goes on…

HOW CAN I USE THIS?

If you use any of the above techniques, then good luck to you. However, don't expect to achieve long-term success or to make many friends in the process.

Alternatively, if you're interested in controlling the negotiation environment in a professional, respectful way, then consider the aspects listed below which can influence or even control the negotiation environment, climate and 'atmosphere'.

Before you do anything, however, you need to ask yourself, 'What sort of climate do I want to create?'

You may want an open, friendly, collaborative, supportive climate, particularly if you're negotiating with long-term partners or you want to encourage the other party to open up and to work with you on problem solving.

Alternatively, you may have an issue to resolve, the other party might have made a mistake or let you down repeatedly, so a more formal, direct, 'down-to-business' or even austere climate may be more in line with your objectives. You can be firm without being nasty to create the right climate to support your goals.

Consider:

- Venue; your premises, their offices, alternating or on neutral territory.
- Dress sense: sending signals about the degree of formality.
- Room layout: in particular, the availability of whiteboard, flipchart, data-projector, etc.
- Furniture: seating and table arrangements, including distance between the various parties, room temperature and ventilation.
- Refreshments: availability and nature of drinks, snacks, lunch, etc.
- Agenda: its nature, formality or rigidity/flexibility in terms of content and time allocation; also, who constructs the agenda – you, them or jointly?
- Greetings: in particular, the length of time it's appropriate to spend on small talk and chit-chat before getting down to business.
- Office tour: to see facilities, offices and to meet other people informally.
- Rapport: the degree to which you build on their comments to build a collaborative supportive climate, or counter them and argue to create a degree of tension/pressure.

- Empathy: the degree to which you consciously build empathy, trust and understanding, or take actions that create and maintain a psychological distance between you and the other party.
- Pace: the speed with which the negotiation proceeds or needs to progress.

3 SCARCITY

3 SCARCITY

Simon was standing in the electrical shop with his son, Adam.

Adam was pleading with his dad to buy him the latest computer games console, but Simon was adamant that he was not going to give in, or at least he certainly wasn't going to get his son the machine today. His thinking was that he could use the incentive of promising to get his son the machine at the end of the month if he was exceptionally good between now and then, kept his room tidy and did some extra jobs around the house.

Then, another man approached from the side, looking at the various games consoles. The man picked up the only remaining box containing the particular machine that Adam was so desperate to have.

Simon froze, feigning interest in the shelves for a moment whilst watching the guy through the corner of his eye; he could see him examining the box.

Unable to stand it any longer than four seconds, Simon turned to the man and said, 'Excuse me, but that's mine.'

'What do you mean it's yours?' responded the 'competing dad'. 'It was on the shelf. I just picked it up.'

'Yes, I know, but I only put it down for a few seconds whilst I checked that I had my credit card – I was about to take it to the till. It's for my son who's here with me – I promised I would buy it for him today.'

A discussion took place but, happily, after 30 seconds the guy handed the box to Simon saying, 'Here, you take it. I can see your son really wants it and the last thing I want to do is to upset him. I can probably get one somewhere else.'

Even more happily, five minutes later Adam was grinning ear-to-ear sitting in his dad's car clutching his brand-new games machine!

INSIGHTS AND LEARNING

Fear of loss is a powerful motivator, as is the fear of losing out on something you want. In fact, psychological and behavioural studies have shown that fear of loss is a much more powerful motivator than the chance of a gain.

Opportunities appear more valuable, and you will work harder to get them when they're less available, rapidly running out or, even worse, as in this example, 'the last one in the shop'.

Imagine you're negotiating to buy a used car. It's the one you want, it meets all your criteria and is a good price. However, you still want to negotiate a €500 discount. The seller says she's reluctant to reduce the price and, in any case, she has two other appointments with potential buyers in the afternoon, so maybe you should call later that evening to see if it is still available. Chances are you will agree to take it now, at full asking price!

Purchasers fear running out of vital component parts as it creates a bottleneck in their production process, and they'll often pay more to secure supply or buy larger quantities. Consumers stockpile basic foodstuffs whenever supply is threatened, and queue for hours at petrol stations when fears of oil supply disruption arise.

After the Icelandic volcano Eyjafjallajökull erupted in 2010, throwing millions of tonnes of ash into the atmosphere and severely disrupting air travel, passengers in Europe were paying up to €3,000 to hire a car – ten times the 'normal' rate.

It's not only about loss or fear of loss though. Hard-to-get things are also perceived as 'better' than easy-to-get things. Discerning consumers will often buy luxury, high cost goods not only for the pleasure of owning such things, but also for the cache of having something that few others can afford – something that they have worked hard to get. Whilst most high-end products do contain quality components, much of their value is intangible. It is 'manufactured' in the mind of the purchaser or owner, by the marketing department. Some watches cost a quarter of a million pounds. Are they really 1,000 times better than a watch that costs £250?

HOW CAN I USE THIS?

If you want to leverage the law of scarcity, show whatever you have in the most tangible way you can; refer to limited resources, stock running out, many other interested buyers, etc.

Impose time limits to increase the perceived value of whatever you're offering or suggesting: *'This offer expires at 6pm today'* or *'The supplier who is first to meet my target buying price will win the contract.'*

If you're selling, build the value of exclusivity in the mind of the purchaser, and what they stand to gain in comparison to others; if not exclusivity of supply then perhaps an early mover advantage, which puts them ahead of the game.

If you're buying, emphasise the value to the supplier of being associated with your organisation and brand, or build the fear in their mind of losing a valuable contract that they currently have.

As a negotiator, by leveraging the instinctive human tendency in the other party to avoid losing something that they already possess, missing out on something that they could have or having something that is rare and/or desirable, you can trigger a psychological and, therefore, a behavioural response that acts in your favour.

4 INTERESTS VS. POSITIONS

4 INTERESTS VS. POSITIONS

Mikkel works for a large company in Copenhagen where he's responsible for buying indirect services such as HR, consultancy and training and development.

For some years now, individual heads of departments have been asking Mikkel to organise outdoor activities for their teams involving off-road vehicles such as buggies, go-karts and ATV's.

Mikkel has been working with the main outdoor activities provider in Denmark, but he finds them to be expensive and not particularly flexible. Also, as the supplier has been progressively putting its prices up, Mikkel has worked hard to find alternative, better-value, typically smaller suppliers.

Unfortunately, an unhealthy pattern has developed in which the dominant provider has been progressively buying up the smaller fledgling suppliers, some of whom Mikkel moved business to, with the result that he's then stuck working with the dominant supplier again, at high prices.

One day, Mikkel had a blinding revelation when Filippa, a colleague, spoke with him:

Filippa: 'Why do you need to keep booking these outdoor team events, Mikkel?'

Mikkel: 'Because the heads of department keep asking for them.'

Filippa: 'Yes, but why do they keep asking for these particular events?'

Mikkel: 'Lots of reasons, I guess… They're fun, they're a form of team-building and motivation, and it inspires the various teams to perform better at work.'

Filippa: 'Does it have to involve off-road vehicles?'

Mikkel: 'What do you mean?'

Filippa: 'Well, if you step back a moment and ask yourself, and the department heads, what it is exactly that they're trying to achieve, would that not give you many other solutions that would meet their needs? For example, if a manager wants to inspire their team, then you could employ a motivational speaker; if they want to build team-working, why not organise internal team games or a quiz after work which will cost virtually nothing? If they want to reward their teams, then why not subsidise a team night out at the local bowling alley at a fraction of the price you're paying the off-road company?'

Until that moment Mikkel had become stuck in his own limited thinking. He had also made a problem for himself because he was not questioning the underlying needs that the department heads wanted to address. Instead of having deeper exploratory conversations with internal stakeholders, he had instead simply acceded to their requests.

From that day forward things changed radically. Over the next few months Mikkel was able to successfully redirect business to a wider range of other external providers. In doing so, he was able to offer managers and their teams a far wider range of options, many of which were more suited to the underlying needs of the teams, and his budget spend halved.

Mikkel also improved his own standing in the company as he was now perceived as an interested internal consultant who was keen to meet the specific needs of each team, rather than what he had been in the past – simply someone who followed instructions and bought the services which departmental heads asked for. He moved from a transactional, unquestioning buyer to a procurement professional who devised and sourced solutions.

INSIGHTS AND LEARNING

An 'interest' a person has in something is not necessarily the same as the 'position' they openly take or state.

In the above case, the departmental heads were taking a 'position', i.e. they were saying specifically what it was that they wanted. A position is something that is obvious, tangible and observable; it can be a proposal, a request, a demand or a number such as 'I don't want to pay more than $9,000.'

However, what underlies a position is an interest. In the above situation, the interests varied between departmental heads, and included things such as reinvigorating the team, rewarding them for a successful project, inspiring them to higher levels of performance, building team spirit, etc. The fact that just one position (an off-road vehicle event) could have very different underpinning interests is the whole point.

You must not assume the interest(s) from the position(s) alone.

HOW CAN I USE THIS?

How you approach a negotiation will play a key role in how the negotiation proceeds. Focusing mostly or only on your position means you're going to be in for a tough battle, and a solution, if any, that is sub-optimal, as neither party has successfully explored each other's interests. Negotiators call this 'leaving money on the table'.

If you stay only at the positions level, such as dealing only with the price of something, then any gain for one person represents a loss for the other. This is called distributive bargaining. It is not sophisticated and one wins at the expense of the other; if I gain a £100 discount, you lose £100 of your profit.

Truly great negotiators focus not on 'dividing the pie' but on 'making the pie bigger'.

Better solutions arise when two parties jointly explore what the other needs from the negotiation and, very importantly, why they need it (the underlying interest). It may be that being paid quicker is more important than absolute price, for example, because the underlying interest at that point of time is cash flow not price.

Think creatively to find a resolution that meets both parties' individual needs and their individual, often different, interests. That said, two negotiators can also share the same interests, for example, finding a mutually acceptable long-term agreement, achieving a speedy resolution, further strengthening the relationship, etc.

So, to find a mutually satisfactory outcome, use questioning and listening, probing and exchanging information to understand the other party's interests (needs) that lie beneath the positions they take, and constantly reinforce your interest(s) to them.

You can also look for low-cost concessions that might have high value to the other person, and vice versa. Get creative; the solutions are there if you jointly explore interests.

5 FROM 'LOSE-LOSE' TO 'WIN-WIN'

5 FROM 'LOSE-LOSE' TO 'WIN-WIN'

David and Julie own a flat, which they have rented out to four different tenants over the past nine years.

After 18 months of happy renting with no issues on either side, their tenants Kim and Ivan contact them to say that, unfortunately, they'll probably need to give notice on the flat soon as they're finding it difficult to pay the monthly rent (£820) due to a downturn in Ivan's business (he's self-employed). They expressed a high degree of regret at having to do this as they have loved living in the flat and would be very sad to leave and move away from neighbours with whom they're good friends. They have two young children at the local primary school.

David and Julie are disappointed to hear the news. Kim and Ivan have been exemplary tenants. They're lovely people and the relationship between all four of them has been extremely positive and strong.

David thanks them for telling them and for giving them advance notice that they're likely to have to move out. David says that he and Julie understand their situation, they'll be very sorry to see them leave, and he'll contact them again in the morning.

If you were David and Julie, what would you do? Your tenants have not yet given notice, but when they do they're only obligated to pay you for one month from that date. What are the key factors or variables in this situation and how could you turn what looks to be heading for a lose-lose situation into a win-win? Think about this now before reading further.

KIM AND IVAN'S PERSPECTIVE

- Very happy in the property, settled and know how everything works in the flat.
- Familiar with the local environment and services, and have made friends with neighbours.
- Have paid the rent in full every month, but now moving into a period of financial uncertainty.
- Moving will incur expense, time to arrange and physically move, contacting all utility suppliers to arrange discontinuation of supply, and arranging for connection of services and transfer of bills in the new property.
- Risk and uncertainty – where will they go, what will their new landlord be like, will the neighbours be horrible, will there be problems with the new flat?
- Disruption to the young children who may have to move schools.

LANDLORD'S PERSPECTIVE

* Inconvenience of having to end the contract and tie up all the loose ends.

* Inconvenience and expense of having to re-advertise the property.

* Risk of having the property empty for some time – it typically takes six weeks to find suitable tenants.

* Risk of not knowing the new tenants and the risk of them turning out to be 'tenants from hell' who do not look after, or even damage, the flat or don't pay their rent on time.

RESOLUTION

The next morning David asked Kim and Ivan to consider carefully their decision, not to rush into it, and to think about some of the issues that might arise that would affect them.

He also stressed that he and Julie would hate to lose them as they have been exemplary tenants and would like to help if they can.

David said that if they still wanted to move then that, of course, is understandable and they'll make it as easy as possible for them. However, if it would help, David was prepared to reduce the monthly rent by £50, with immediate effect, if they were to sign a contract extension for the next 1+6 months.

Kim and Ivan thanked David and said they would talk about it that evening.

The next morning Kim and Ivan telephoned to say that they would be delighted to accept the gesture to reduce the rent and, yes, they would sign a new contract for the next seven months.

INSIGHTS AND LEARNING

This true story has a good ending. The tenants are relieved and happy, and in fact would probably have had far more expense, risk and uncertainty by moving. Therefore, by accepting the £50 per month saving they're now better off.

The landlords would have lost money through the cost of changing, the risk of weeks of lost income without a tenant and high uncertainty about the new tenants. They now know that rather than having tenants on a one-month contract, they can be assured of regular income for the next seven months. If the flat had been un-let for just two weeks, then the lost income alone would be £410. It would have taken more than eight months at a £50 reduction to recoup this, and that does not include the hassle and cost of finding new tenants.

But, it's not only about money. This case has a happy ending because everyone is happy and the relationships are even stronger – a true win-win in which all parties cooperated and tried to work creatively to find a mutually positive solution.

However, what if the situation were different? What if a lose-lose really was likely, perhaps because one or both parties are not being reasonable? What could you do in that situation?

HOW CAN I USE THIS IN MORE TRICKY SITUATIONS?

There are many advantages to aiming for and achieving a 'win-win' solution. However, you may find yourself in a situation where the other party, for whatever reason, doesn't seem to want to achieve a collaborative solution.

In such cases conflict can escalate, the atmosphere becomes charged with emotions, communication channels close down or are used to criticise and blame the other party, and the focus may shift towards attack and defence.

The original issues can become blurred and/or new issues are added as the conflict becomes personalised. Perceived differences become magnified as each side gets locked into their initial positions and resorts to lies, threats, distortions or other attempts to force the other party to comply with demands.

In such situations you (and others) need to open up lines of communication, build trust and focus on cooperativeness. But what practically can you do to shift towards a 'win-win'?

- Let the other side 'vent' and acknowledge the other's views, listen actively, and respond calmly and professionally.
- Rephrase the other's comments to make sure you hear them; reflect back your understanding of the other's views.
- Increase the accuracy of communication; listen hard in the middle of conflict.
- Build on what you have in common; because conflict tends to magnify perceived differences, you need to look for and highlight similarities and common goals: *'It's in both of our interests to find a solution here.'*
- Control and dissect concerns; break larger issues into smaller pieces.
- Find a common 'enemy'; or highlight the consequences for both parties of not reaching an agreement.
- Depersonalise the conflict; separate the issues/problems from the people.
- Make proposals/suggestions that the other party can easily say 'yes' to; if it would help, consider making a small concession as a sign of good faith.

- Reformulate solutions; repackage the deal, emphasise the positives of their acceptance and make it more palatable to swallow.

- Find legitimate objective criteria, or third party reference points/information, in order to impartially evaluate and justify the solution you propose.

6 BOILING FROG

6 BOILING FROG

Supplier: 'Sarah, I've included in the email our fees for the coming year's continuation of contract.'

Sarah: 'Yes, I saw that, but you did not make it clear to me in previous discussions the fact that you're suggesting an 11% increase in fees, which I consider to be totally unacceptable and, frankly, inexplicable.'

Supplier: 'The thing is, we've had additional costs imposed on our business this year, and even though 11% might sound a little on the upside, it's totally in line with what we charge our other clients.'

Sarah: 'OK – two things. Firstly, I did a bit of digging around and I've looked at the fee rates that you've been charging us for the last four years. We've had some personnel changes over that period and so it seems to me that along with our discontinuity of purchasing contact person there has been a series of excessive fee increases from your side. In years 1–2 you increased your fees by 6%, the following year it was a 7% increase, the year after that it was 9% and now, in the year that I've taken over, you're proposing 11%. Compounded over a four-year period that's a 37% increase. The compounded inflation rate over that period has been less than 10%. How do you justify these massive increases?'

'And... before you answer that, my second point is that whatever input costs you have in your own business model are your concern not mine; and if you're accepting an 11% increase for your own input costs, then you probably need to go back and renegotiate with your own suppliers. I would not accept it and I am not accepting it in this case from you.'

Supplier: 'I do see your position, Sarah, but you need to understand that when we negotiated the original contract with one of your predecessors, we did it at a very low price. We've got to get back to our normal market rates.'

Sarah: 'You were clearly happy to agree the contract five years ago, so it must have made good business sense for you then. It seems to me that you've been ratcheting up the fees in the last four years, well above the rate of inflation, and you're now just relying on us rolling over the contract at your new rates. Well, it's not going to happen.'

Supplier: 'I'm sorry Sarah. I can't really do much about the fees and, in any case, there is quite a lot of work that you will need us to do this year, so maybe we can just get to the end of this year and then we can see what we can do fee-wise at that point?'

Sarah: *'I'll tell you what, I will make your job easier. I can save you a whole lot of trouble. We will not renew the contract. We have other highly respected suppliers lined up who are ready to start next month, who have quoted fees that are 30% below yours. I'm sorry it had to end this way but, whether you intended it or not, you've priced yourselves progressively out of business.'*

INSIGHTS AND LEARNING

It doesn't sound nice but a 'boiling frog' is just a metaphor, not an act of reptilian cruelty.

The term comes from the (alleged) fact that if you put a frog into a pan of water, and very slowly turn up the heat, the frog would be unable to detect the gradual rise in temperature and so stays put until it dies. Don't try this at home!

A 'boiling frog' in negotiation terms refers to the tactic of gradually turning up the 'heat' in a negotiation, so that the unpleasantness is spread over time, rather than coming as a big shock at one moment.

In the situation above, it was a case of progressively ratcheting up the percentage of the annual price increase, without even putting an annual price renegotiation on the agenda. It's remarkable how the supplier got away with it for several years. This could be explained by taking advantage of the constant changing of purchasing staff on the customer's side (a level of understandable, but not forgivable, ignorance) and/or relying on the inertia of rolling contracts that are easier for customers to re-agree to than to go to the trouble of sourcing alternative suppliers.

Purchasers take note: incumbent suppliers rely a great deal on inertia and becoming 'locked in' as a legacy supplier.

Another version of the boiling frog is to introduce something that is unpalatable or unpleasant by offering to phase it in over time. Alternatively, it can involve phasing out over time a previously agreed benefit, or something else that is desirable. The theory is that the pain is delayed or easier to take in stages, or by the time the change comes into effect the agreeing person will have moved on.

Governments often announce tax increases or benefits cuts, but state that they'll be delayed by 12 months, or they'll be tapered or phased in; they want to avoid a short-term revolt and delay the 'pain' to a point in time when most people will have forgotten about it or any momentum to protest will have been lost.

Sales people may use this technique as an incentive to create movement; for example, by offering 0% finance terms, or 'low-start' stepped payments if the customer agrees the deal today. They know the pain to the customer, and the benefit to them, will come later. The customer often feels that they're getting a good deal today and they can worry about paying for it later.

HOW CAN I USE THIS?

Awareness of what's going on is half of the solution to the 'boiling frog'.

As a general point, and something to keep at the front of your mind as you read this book, is that when you're aware of what's happening, any tactic loses most, if not all, of its power.

If you're happy with a phased introduction or removal of whatever is being negotiated, then it could actually be to your advantage to agree; so long as you realise (and are accepting of) the fact that such arrangements usually end up costing you more in the long run. Maybe cash flow for you is tight right now but you know things are improving in a few months, so it is in your interests to agree to be boiled in the short term!

Maybe you suspect you're being 'screwed' with a contract, but you know you have a 12-month get-out clause which you can enact at any time, and probably intend to, as you're secretly working on an alternative solution?

However, if you suspect that you're being deliberately drip-fed a stream of small pieces of bad news, which have a compounding effect, then you can express frustration that each time you have a conversation there's yet another issue.

You could state categorically that before continuing you need absolute clarity about the full scope and depth of what needs to be discussed, and point out that you suspect a 'war of attrition' or 'death by a thousand cuts'.

Yes, some of these expressions are gritty, controversial or even confrontational, but if you're being manipulated, you need to expose dirty tactics, give the other party a chance to refute them or use some of your own.

As illustrated in the case, you could point out the size of the gap between where you started and where you are now, and that a series of small changes over time have now created a compounded situation that is no longer acceptable to you. This is factual, objective, non-emotional and difficult to argue with. It also means that you can continue or, indeed, end the contract, if needed, whilst preserving some degree of relationship.

Say *'Enough is enough'* and you will now withdraw from the negotiation. Maybe they have more to lose than you, so now's the time to test it out!

7 THE POWER OF SILENCE

7 THE POWER OF SILENCE

'Hi, mate. We've fitted all the upstairs carpets, but we've got a problem with the final bedroom. The piece the warehouse has supplied is 1 inch too short. Sorry about that, but we'll have to take it back and get a new piece cut.'

Graham, the house owner, was annoyed about this, but rather than get angry he decided to try to make the situation work for him. He asked the carpet fitters to leave the carpet piece at the house and he would revisit the carpet showroom. What follows is the conversation between Graham and the showroom salesman.

Graham:	'Hi, your carpet fitters have done a great job with the hall, stairs, landing and all of the upstairs rooms except one. They're unable to fit the carpet in the final bedroom because it has been cut too short.'
Salesman:	'I'm sorry, sir. That shouldn't have happened. Let me arrange for a new piece to be cut at the factory and shipped to us as soon as possible.'
Graham:	'What are you going to do with the piece that has been cut wrongly? It's a very unusual shape so it's unlikely someone is going to have a room shaped like that.'
Salesman:	'Well, we'll put it back into stock and see if we can sell it as an offcut.'
Graham:	'Well, I've got one room downstairs where I could use that piece. I was not planning on re-carpeting that room but if I trim the odd-shaped piece, I reckon I can get it to fit because the room is smaller. I'd be prepared to buy the piece off you but obviously at a significantly reduced price.'
Salesman:	'OK, sir. That carpet piece was supplied to you at £190, and it was already in the sale, as you know. If you wanted to keep it, I could take another 20% off, so you can have it for £150.'
Graham:	'Sorry, that's not going to work. It's not a good enough deal for me and if you take it back, you're going to have the hassle and cost of picking it up, re-stocking it, holding it in your store, trying to sell a very oddly-shaped piece to someone else and then having to re-deliver it. You're probably going to have to discount it far more than 20% to be able to sell it to someone else. I was thinking of £50. Will you take £50 to get it off your hands and as a gesture to me for the inconvenience this has caused?'
Salesman:	'Whoa, that's totally impossible. I might be able to take a little more off the price, but I cannot get anywhere close to £50.'

The salesman takes out a calculator, punches in some numbers and then says that the best he can do is £110 – he can go no lower as that is his cost price.

Graham: *'I appreciate you moving on the price, but my offer is £50. I can give you the cash now and we can both move on.'*

Now comes the interesting bit. The salesman takes out his calculator again and proceeds to punch more numbers. This goes on for some time. Meanwhile, Graham stays completely silent. He notices that the salesman's hand has started to shake; he's avoiding eye contact and seems transfixed on his calculator. The silence continues and, whilst Graham feels he should say something, he knows about the power of silence so he lets the silence work for him.

However, despite holding off for probably 30 seconds – which due to the pressure would have felt like half an hour – Graham decided that he had probably pushed the guy to his limit. (Graham could see the salesman was under some considerable distress – shaking, red in the face and with moisture appearing on his brow.) In any case, he was happy to pay £110 for the carpet as it would normally cost him £300 to carpet the downstairs room.

Graham eventually broke the silence by saying, *'Look, it's not worth arguing over.'*

He was about to follow this with, *'I'm prepared to pay you the £110'*, but he was interrupted by the salesman who immediately blurted out, *'Yes, you're right. It's not worth arguing – you can have it for £50.'*

INSIGHTS AND LEARNING

Most people are uncomfortable with silence… they feel they have to fill it.

Unfortunately, when negotiating, often what they fill it with weakens their position. Some people find it so uncomfortable and excruciatingly embarrassing that they stuff any silence with devastating and unnecessary concessions.

At an important client meeting a key account manager had just made a superb presentation. The audience were impressed, but an uneasy silence developed as they looked at each other to see who was going to be the first to speak.

Just as one interested person was about to ask a question, the presenter jumped into the silence by going over his key points again, hoping that by reinforcing his message this would somehow double the impact.

The power and the moment were both lost. If he had kept his mouth firmly closed, smiled, looked around the room and invited questions from his audience, the outcome might have been different.

The deal *was* rescued, but only after much effort and awkwardness.

So, try not to be the first person to fill the silence void, especially when you have just made a proposal or asked a question. Other people may simply be thinking (which is what you should also be doing) and considering their response – give them space; give them time.

HOW CAN I USE THIS?

- Hold your nerve; put a pleasant expression on your face, and wait… and wait… and wait…

- Use the 'broken record' technique (see Part Two) to restate your question or demand and wait for a response from the other party – it's their turn to speak, after all.

- Try rephrasing your statement, request or question in a different way, but do not be deviated from your line of enquiry or intention.

- Be more direct – tell the other party that you would appreciate a response to your last statement/question.

- Ask them how you should interpret their silence?

- Interpret their silence to your advantage as in: *'I'm taking your lack of response to this as acceptance of the point/a lack of interest/open to further discussion'* – whichever suits you best. It's then up to them to refute this, and to do so they'll have to break the silence.

8 THREAT OF SUBSTITUTION

8 THREAT OF SUBSTITUTION

Charles: (A Senior Buyer of metal packaging.) *'Hi Andrew, as we're coming to the end of our three-year supply agreement, we need to renegotiate the way forward. As you know, the oil price has almost halved in the last nine months and this is causing us to rethink how we package our end products in the future.'*

Andrew: (A Senior Key Account Manager for a major metal supplier.) *'Charles, I've been anticipating this conversation, not so much to do with the oil price, which as you will imagine does not impact on us directly in terms of raw material costs, but of course because our current agreement is up for renewal.'*

Charles: *'Andrew, we spend close to $100 million per year on metal packaging alone, and you know that you have about a third of that market with us, so our spend with you, and with our other suppliers is significant. You and I have a very strong relationship, at least six years now, and our respective companies, have been trading together for more than 20 years. But I'm finding myself in a very difficult position. The situation with the dramatic drop in oil prices means that alternative packaging options are now becoming increasingly attractive to us, in particular plastic packaging substitutes. You see where I'm coming from?'*

Andrew: *'Absolutely, Charles. Neither of us control the oil price, and neither of us are experts in plastic packaging, but I see your point. Of course, it would be a massive internal decision for you to decide to switch from metal to plastic, and who knows what will happen to the oil price in future? It could be back up to previous levels within a year, or even higher, so you clearly will need to factor that risk into any internal decision you make. I would counsel against making a hasty judgment on this one, especially as you say, the amount of money involved is large.'*

Charles: *Andrew, the analysts are predicting that the oil price will remain at or around these levels for at least the next two years, and may then continue at that level. Yes, I know we can't predict the future, but if we take their advice, it would be wise for us to at least move some of our packaging to plastics. If this dramatic fall in oil price had not happened, then we would not be having this type of conversation, but put yourself in my shoes, I have to make strategic and tactical decisions that are best for my company. Also, I'm not comparing you at the moment with other metal*

Andrew:	*suppliers, my comparison is between metal and plastic – so it's a totally different scenario.'*
Andrew:	I understand. Can we meet up in the next few days and talk about how we move forwards?'
Charles:	'Absolutely, I'm free all of next Thursday if you can come in.'

INSIGHTS AND LEARNING

This is a complex case – one that's evolving at the time of writing.

The outcome is as yet undetermined, but in terms of insights and learning, despite what ultimately transpires, we can take a great deal from this situation. By adding in a little more 'insider' information we can note the following:

- The power of the relationship – both personally between Charles and Andrew and the longevity of the trading relationship between the two companies – is strong and the situation is strategic, so it seems likely that both parties are going to want to collaborate to find a way to keep the relationship and the contract in place.

- This is not metal vs. metal, it's metal vs. a totally different commodity and industry, so the competitive landscape changes dramatically. Suddenly, the metal provider has to think beyond his traditional competitors. The threat of substitution radically changes the game.

- The huge amount of annual spend means that any changes the customer makes will have a dramatic effect, positive or negative, on their own business. Likewise, the implications for the supplier of losing, reducing or compromising the profit on the contract are going to be substantial.

- When the external environment changes significantly the negotiation situation changes dramatically. There are many external factors and forces that are not controllable. The key is to be agile, creative and to be able to respond quickly and effectively.

- When two parties are facing a third, external change, they probably need to collaborate to work out a win-win, almost as though the external factor was their common 'enemy', with them working in partnership to overcome this unforeseen event, trend or force.

- The risk of shifting from metal to plastic would be high. Even though Charles could make massive cost savings in the short-term, these could not be guaranteed in the future, and so it could mean swinging from one packaging type to the other and then back again, with all of the cost implications those moves and changes imply.

- Charles also needs to take into account the substantial switching costs that are outside of his remit. Many costs may not fall within his budget but would impact on other internal stakeholders, such as the production facility, warehousing, sales and marketing teams, product returns department… to name just a few.

- Andrew is fearful of losing a massive, long-term contract. He needs to think creatively about what he can do to retain, secure and even grow this contract.

- Charles privately knows that he can only switch 25% of the metal business to plastic within the next 12 months. So, whilst he has leverage over Andrew, he knows it is not unlimited, and any switchover would need to be phased in.

- Charles also knows, however, that if he can gain a significant price reduction on metal packaging from Andrew, then not only will that help him secure substantial savings immediately, without the hassle of switching some business to plastic, he can then also use that secured cost reduction as a strong and legitimate bargaining chip with his other two metal suppliers to get them to make a similar price reduction or face losing the business.

- Andrew is seeing the oil price reduction impacting him in terms of his negotiations with other customers. He now has over-capacity because of the rise in attractivness of plastic packaging and he knows that he has to make a significant downwards price move otherwise he stands to lose out big time to the plastic and other metal manufacturers.

- Andrew knows that his company benefited several years ago when the market shifted from plastic to metal. So, whilst his fear is that the shift will now go the other way, he can hardly complain as the logic works both ways and he has lived off the profits in the meantime!

- Charles has already decided upon a % price reduction that he would be happy with and which he thinks is fair, taking into account all of his switching costs and knock-on complications of switching. Hopefully the two of them can come to a fair and reasonable agreement within the next few weeks.

HOW CAN I USE THIS?

- Whether you're a supplier or a customer, never become complacent. The customer may decide to suspend or terminate business with a supplier but, equally, a supplier may decide, for multiple reasons, to stop supply. It's not uncommon for purchasers to forget this, thinking that because they're the ones with the money they hold most of the power – often they don't.

- Keep your eyes and ears to the market, and particularly watch out for emerging trends that might indicate that totally different solutions could eliminate what you offer or what you need to buy. Think photographic film vs.

digital photography, paper vs. electronic storage, flying to business meetings vs. video conferencing, travelling to an office vs. working flexibly from home, or sitting in your shorts and T-shirt on the top of a hill… the list is endless.

- For strategic long-term relationships, those in which you're mutually dependent, you need to be as close as is professionally possible to the people on the other side. Trust, disclosure, honesty, information sharing, etc. should be high and, of course, mutually exchanged, otherwise it's not a true partnership.

- When faced with an external potentially disruptive change, then a strong partnering relationship will enable you to join forces against the 'common enemy' and come up with creative solutions that are beneficial to both parties.

- Step back and out of the negotiation for a while and consider what some of the 'unintended consequences' (see Part Two) might be of what is proposed, not only to you, but also to other internal stakeholders and/or external parties. Take these into account before agreeing a final deal.

- If you're feeling particularly combative, and you're in a strong position, consider using one incumbent party's concession as a challenge for other similar suppliers to meet the same conditions, or risk losing their current share of the business. Alternatively, use it as a threshold for other potential suppliers to cross if they want the chance of winning the business.

- Power is powerful, but truly professional, principled negotiators do not flaunt or abuse their power; they use it in order to build their confidence. They make the other party subtly aware that they hold a certain position, but they do not ram it down their throats – the power balance is often implied and implicit, it does not necessarily need to be put on the table in a blunt or brutal way.

9 USING THREAT

9 USING THREAT

On the eight-hour late evening flight from Qatar to London, Frank had been fortunate to be upgraded to business class. Normally his company only pays for economy.

Frank was looking forward to the luxury, service, food and fine wine, the restful half-empty cabin and the chance to get a good night's sleep.

Before take-off he noticed a Saudi gentleman standing in the business class section speaking with three ladies, all of whom were dressed in black – they were his three wives. The charming thing about this situation was that it was clear the Saudi man had paid for his wives to travel business class while he sat further back in economy. He remained in the business class section for 20–30 minutes, conversing with his wives, and as soon as the fasten seatbelt sign illuminated and the pilot announced the plane would be taking off he returned to his allotted seat behind the curtain.

Unfortunately, our Saudi gentleman did not seem able to stay in his economy seat for too long. Repeatedly during the flight he would slip through the curtain and find some reason to speak to his wives, often for 20+ minutes. This happened several times and about a third of the way into the flight his tactics became bolder. First, he would sit on the arm of an adjacent vacant business class seat whilst he conversed with his wives. The next time, he would sit on the arm and then slip into the seat itself, and remain there until asked to go back by a member of cabin crew. On two further occasions he entered the cabin and sat in vacant seats near the back that were less obvious to the cabin crew, and when one of them approached he 'pretended' to be filling in some sort of travel documentation.

The air stewardess tried on multiple occasions to ask the gentleman to return to his seat as he was not entitled to travel in business class, and, in any case, his frequent incursions were disrupting the service and potentially disturbing other passengers.

Frank observed these frequent altercations and particularly the Saudi man's resistance and reluctance to return to his seat. Even when he did return to the economy cabin, within 10 minutes he was back in business class. The air stewardess was now getting really annoyed, but she did not seem able to persuade him.

At this point Frank unbuckled his belt, climbed out of his fully flat bed, walked over to the gentleman, puffed out his chest, stood as tall as he could and said in a loud and commanding voice:

'Sir, I am an Air Marshall. You have no right to sit in this cabin, and you must obey the

requests and orders of air cabin crew at all times. Not to do so is against international air law and can potentially result in imprisonment. I am giving you a first and final warning. Go back to your seat and do not enter this cabin again. Do I make myself clear?'

The Saudi nodded, immediately got up, returned to his seat and was not seen again.

Frank was a mattress salesman.

INSIGHTS AND LEARNING

Firstly, understand that the use of threat, or 'implied threat', is a legitimate negotiation tactic. However, like anything with immense force, such as a hammer, it needs to be handled carefully, and… you can damage yourself in the process!

Imagine if the Saudi had demanded to see documentation of the 'Air Marshall's' credentials or, even worse, started pushing him around the cabin.

This case highlights:

- The power of a threat to cause the other party to take the action you demand.
- The importance of not letting you, or others, be pushed around with unreasonable, unfair or objectionable behaviour.
- Standing up for your rights, what is right and the rights of others.
- The fact that a threat can work in a one-shot, one-time situation where an ongoing relationship is unlikely or not required.
- The power of perceived authority.
- The power of referencing regulations and laws.
- The fact that, in some cultures, a man will not listen to, respect or obey a woman, but he will listen to, respect and obey another man.

HOW CAN I USE THIS?

Understand these critical aspects about threats:

- They can have both intended and unintended consequences; so be careful.
- For a threat to have legitimacy, and for you to have credibility in wielding it, you need to be prepared to follow through with action; otherwise do not threaten.
- You need to have built a track record that shows that when you've threatened an action in the past you have carried it out; this confers proven legitimacy.
- It may be that you threaten to carry out an action, such as impose a sanction

or to 'walk away'; you threaten to remove something beneficial such as next year's contract, or you simply remind the other party that you'll remember what they've done, thereby threatening some form of, as yet undefined, future negative payback.

- You need to be sure that your organisation will back you, otherwise the other party may find a way around you, making you look weak and ineffectual.

- Threats can result in deadlock, hostility and a 'lose-lose' situation; are you prepared for this eventuality and, if so, are you capable of dealing with it?

- Threats can damage relationships; people have long memories, you may win a short-term 'battle' only to lose the more important 'campaign' or eventual 'war'.

- Threats can work for one-off transactions or short-term negotiations; they're rarely appropriate in long-term strategic relationships.

A common threat is to walk away or to threaten to do so. However, if it's obvious that it's in your best interests to walk away, then the other party may wonder why you've not done so already? So, the other party has to believe that if it's in your best interests you will walk away. If they do not, then the threat is empty and they may call your bluff.

Rather than making overt threats, a better strategy may be to hint at a negative consequence. For example: *'Paula, you have put me in a very difficult position. I really don't want to have to look for alternative suppliers. However, if you're determined to hold your position, then you leave me no choice.'*

Finally, giving in to threats can set a dangerous precedent and paradoxically portray you as weak. Hold your ground if you can, appeal to reason and walk away yourself, whilst 'keeping the door open' for the other party should things change.

10 QUOD ERAT DEMONSTRANDUM (QED)

10 QUOD ERAT DEMONSTRANDUM (QED)

Mentor: *'Stefan, it's not often I have a conversation quite as direct as this, but on this occasion I feel it's warranted. I've been employed by your organisation to help coach you and other members of the team, to help you all work together more effectively.*

So far, being totally honest with you, I have found every member of the team to be cooperative and willing to consider the suggestions I've made; a good deal of progress has been made. There is just one exception, and that person is you.

You and I have had three one-to-one meetings now, and on each occasion I feel we've not made much, if any, progress. Almost every time I make a suggestion you rebut it, give me a reason why it is invalid or won't work. I find you arrogant, stubborn and, frankly, I don't think anyone can help you – I think your arrogance is getting in your own way.'

Stefan: *'Yeah, and your problem is <u>what</u> exactly?'*

Mentor: *'QED Stefan – goodbye.'*

INSIGHTS AND LEARNING

A super-sized ego can be tough for others to deal with, whether they're in your own organisation, a supplier or a customer with whom you are negotiating.

Egomaniacs can actually be super-effective and successful. Their ego may be based on an outstanding record of achievement, expertise or capability. However, it would be nice if they retained those admirable aspects whilst toning down the less attractive bits. But if they won't change themselves, what can you do?

HOW CAN I USE THIS?

- Remember, nobody's perfect; everyone has flaws and weaknesses – yes, even you! However, egomaniacs may dismiss such flaws, admit them but say they're irrelevant, or say that other people should recognise their towering strengths and tolerate any flaws as the price to pay for excellence! Do not allow this. Say something like: *'Yes, you're the top sales performer for three years running, but look at the trail of destruction and bad feelings you leave in your wake?'*

- Most dominant people respect dominance in others. Even if they don't agree with what's being said, they often respect those who stand up for themselves and for what they believe.

- Dominant people often look down on those who they perceive to be weak or too soft – those who give in easily. However, the domineering person uses the perceived weaknesses of others (whatever they are) to further reinforce their own 'strength' relative to those people, which further reinforces their attitude of indomitability. Don't tolerate being talked down to, talked over, or treated in any way other than professionally and respectfully; push back.

- Perhaps these ego-monsters are so self-absorbed they don't realise the negative impact they have on others; they simply don't think, or they lack emotional intelligence. It's no excuse. Talk to them about the difference between 'impact' and 'intention' (see Part Two), allowing them to save face by stating that you're certain they do not intend to create the impression they do, yet that is how they come across to you and to others. Give them an opportunity to change.

- Alternatively, could they be living in a 'feedback vacuum'? If they're very senior, then people around them may be afraid to criticise. In the absence of feedback to the contrary, they start to believe their own self-adulating press. Consider initiating a 360-degree feedback process, in which they, and others, take part.

- Make them see the negative consequences for them in the broader or longer term of continuing to behave in this egotistical manner, and the benefits to them of consciously moderating their behaviour in future.

- Mention the unmentionable; speak up and talk about the 'elephant in the room' that nobody else will raise. It may be painful, but you may achieve a breakthrough.

- If all else fails, and you're lucky enough not to need to negotiate with such people, then walk away – professionally. You're better than them, and it's their loss not yours.

11 COGNITIVE DISSONANCE

11 COGNITIVE DISSONANCE

On the second day of a three-day internal business meeting in Shanghai, Fritz walked proudly into the room with a big smile on his face. There were about 16 local Chinese delegates involved in the meeting and Fritz, from the corporate head office in Frankfurt, was the only 'foreigner', visiting China on business for the first time.

'Hey, Fritz! You look happy!' shouted one of the Chinese delegates.

'You bet,' responded Fritz. 'It's my son's birthday next week and I've managed to buy him a pair of roller boots in the market that I know he's going to love, and I got them at a great price.'

'That's great,' said another. 'How much did you pay?'

In the next two seconds Fritz experienced a traumatic emotional plunge, from previously being delighted and very pleased with his performance, to feeling cheated, resentful and angry.

You can guess why that happened. It does not need to be spelled out.

Fritz remained resentful and annoyed for the remainder of the day. The incident affected his mood and his contributions (or relative lack of) during the meeting. Even though he was a mature, experienced negotiator, for some reason he could not seem to shake off the fact that he felt he had been conned by the market trader and he could have got a better deal.

What makes this even more weird is that Fritz is used to negotiating deals involving millions of Euros, and yet a relatively trifling amount for a pair of roller boots had such a negative psychological impact on him.

The good news from this story is that his son got the roller boots that he wanted, he was delighted, and he loved his dad even more for it.

INSIGHTS AND LEARNING

Cognitive dissonance refers to a situation where you feel a tension or disconnect between what you think happened, what actually happened, what you think or the facts of the situation.

In this case, Fritz was more than happy with the outcome of his negotiation. In fact, he was delighted. What changed was that he was then presented with a reaction and information from others that violently caused him to reappraise the situation and outcome. It was literally seconds from triumph to disaster; delight to despair; feeling assured to ashamed.

In the negotiation world this phenomenon can translate into what's called 'post-purchase cognitive dissonance reduction'. Apart from being a wonderful expression to casually trip off your tongue at parties, it describes the tendency of a person to justify to themselves, and to others, why they made the 'right' decision when making a major purchase.

We've all done it. We've all bought something, or made a major public commitment, and even if seeds of doubt then start to germinate, we continue to justify why we have made the 'right' decision. Yes... we lie to ourselves. How stupid is that?

In '1 Logic vs. Emotion', we briefly refer to this natural human tendency in the example of trying to justify to your partner why you made an impulse car purchase. However, this case is different. It's not about making an impulse purchase — the price of which was fair and you're still happy with — it's about what happens at a psychological level when you think you've negotiated a good deal and then some information comes to light that disabuses you of that thought.

Maybe it's new information or, even worse, maybe it was there all along but you did not do your research or due diligence to uncover it, and you now feel foolish, angry with yourself, conned or some other negative emotion.

Imagine two couples who do not know each other meeting for the first time on day one of a two-week cruise. Before long the conversation turns to what good value the trip is. Inevitably, figures are bandied around and it then becomes painfully obvious that one couple have paid a lot less than the other for exactly the same holiday. One couple feel delightedly smug. The other couple feel like jumping off the ship.

Forget a cheap pair of roller boots. If you're human, knowing someone else is getting the same as you and they paid $800 less per person will irritate you for days.

So what value can we take from this true-life roller boots case and these anecdotes?

HOW CAN I USE THIS?

Firstly, you owe it to yourself, and others, to do your research and due diligence. Knowledge is power and having as much information, benchmarking, third-party insights, etc. upfront is like gold dust.

Know your target(s), your limits and work hard to discover the ZOPA (Zone Of Potential Agreement) - see Part Two.

Obviously, you want to negotiate the very best deal you can, and you can usually tell when you've pushed someone close to his or her limits. Be content with this.

Don't try to squeeze out that very last cent. You're probably doing more damage than you're gaining. It's taking you longer and probably building resentment from the other side.

If the deal falls within what you were initially prepared to accept, then what's the problem? You achieved what you set out to achieve, so don't beat yourself up unnecessarily about it.

Difficult though it might be to swallow, you are where you are. At the time you considered it to be 'good business', so hang on to that thought and don't make things worse or sabotage things further. Roll with it and learn, learn, learn for next time – so you salvage a positive lesson from a less than ideal historical situation.

Sometimes it's better not to know and to get on and enjoy the look on your son's face or the holiday cruise. After all, you were happy to pay those prices at the time so why let what you now discover spoil the whole experience? If you don't want to know, maybe you shouldn't ask.

12 BRINKMANSHIP

12 BRINKMANSHIP

Derek was a difficult character. The senior managers of his company, who had two manufacturing plants in the north-east of England, were tired of his belligerent attitude. Eventually, they found what they thought was a legitimate reason to dismiss him.

The problem was that Derek was popular amongst the workers. He was an active union member and had been working for the company for more than 30 years – he was part of the institution – everyone knew Derek.

When hearing of Derek's imminent dismissal, the union at plant 1 threatened a walkout of the 350 unionised production staff. They imposed a deadline of Derek being reinstated by 11am the following morning, otherwise there would be a mass walkout and the plant would have to close down.

The company called the union's bluff – they did not believe they would follow through on their threat.

At 11am the next day 350 workers walked out – the plant came to a standstill. The workers did not get paid for six days and they became increasingly angry. The company encountered some stock shortages, but as it had another plant 25 miles away, and they had sufficient warehouse stock, they were able to keep most of their customers supplied during the shutdown.

Who wins in this situation?

Was it Derek?

In one sense, yes. Derek pocketed more than £20,000 as a 'settlement' – a payment to encourage him to 'leave quietly' and not cause any trouble. But what about everyone else?

All 350 of his former colleagues went back to work on day seven, each having lost a week's pay – that amounted to much more than £20,000. They had not achieved what they wanted (Derek's reinstatement) and the company had to recover from a whole week's production shutdown.

But did Derek really win?

No. He had a big wad of cash in his pocket, but he lost a lot of friends and supporters in the process. Many of the workers felt and thought that their walkout was a show of massive support for one of their colleagues/comrades. So, when Derek accepted the company 'deal', his former colleagues and union boss, Steve, realised that the only losers in this situation were themselves. Derek was ostracised and lost many long-term friends in the process. Derek was £20,000 richer and 350 friends poorer.

What was the company's perspective on this?

They were happy.

They had stood up to the union, which they had found to be increasingly militant in recent years. The payment to Derek was a fraction of what it would have cost if they had gone to court and, whilst production was halted, the stock outages were not bad enough to cause supply chain problems. Very importantly, the company wanted to use this situation as a way to show they were prepared to stand up to an increasingly quarrelsome union. They would not be pushed to the edge, nor threatened with being pushed over the edge.

The following year the two production plants were consolidated into one. Guess which one was closed down?

INSIGHTS AND LEARNING

The company called the union's bluff. They did not think that 350 workers would walk out because of one man – but they did. The company lost six day's production, but did not have to pay wages for those six days so the loss was not so great as it could have been. They had stock in the warehouse and another manufacturing plant within 25 miles. The company considered the eventual outcome as satisfactory – a price worth paying.

The union boss, Steve, lost face – he now felt impotent rather than important; embarrassed rather than empowered.

The workers lost 350 x 6 days' pay – they felt aggrieved towards their employer, towards their union boss and towards Derek.

Derek got a nice pay-off. After things had settled down he received a call from Steve, the union rep. He answered the call as he took another sip of chilled white wine on the balcony of his new apartment in Malaga.

Derek: 'Hi Steve, good to hear from you… How's it going?'
Steve: 'F*&% off!'

HOW CAN I USE THIS?

Brinkmanship means going right to the edge in terms of either pushing an issue as far as possible, or in refusing to agree a deal as a seemingly fixed deadline approaches.

It relies a great deal on bluff, and on who can hold out the longest. The hope from the party playing this tactic is that the other side will give in first. In this case the union didn't think the company would sack Derek; the company didn't think the union would walk out.

Brinkmanship is a risky game and it requires a great deal of skill and nerve to avoid falling over the brink, resulting in a lose-lose outcome.

If you do wish to use this as a negotiation tactic, then try to get the other party to see the 'edge' as being closer than it actually is; perhaps you have imposed an artificially close deadline when in fact you have more time. Alternatively, confidently state that you will indeed carry out the threat. Say something like, *'If you don't believe we will take that action, then try us. We will show you what we're capable of doing.'*

However, bluffing is a risky game and if you're going to bluff, you need to know what you will do if your bluff is called.

When faced with a brinkmanship approach what do you do?

- First, hold your nerve. Do not allow yourself to become rattled; remain cool and calm.

- If the nature of the tactic is an imposed deadline, try to signal that you have plenty of time and that, if needed, you can negotiate more time for yourself internally/externally (which may or may not be the case).

- If the other party asks for a decision today, say something like, *'Okay, if you want my decision today, then I will give it to you. My decision is "no". If you want a different decision, then you need to give me more time.'*

- However, be careful in counter-bluffing; it may result in a lose-lose stand-off, or you may end up the overall loser, as was the case with the 350 workers and union boss.

- If it is the other party's imposed deadline, then simply point out to them that their deadline is approaching. It's not your deadline; you did not impose it, they did.

- Suggest to the other party that to prevent them from rushing too hastily into an ill thought out deal, they renegotiate the timescale themselves, or buy more time from their side.

- Indicate that if the deadline really is non-negotiable, then, sadly, on this occasion, it would appear that it won't be possible to achieve a negotiated agreement within their time frame. You appreciate that they're under time pressure, but that's not your problem.

There are also lessons in this case about allegiance, collaboration and values.

When offered a 'stack of cash' Derek's previous values seemed to evaporate. He chose money over relationships and, whilst he then moved to a more comfortable life, we wonder how he now feels about his colleagues, all 350 of whom supported him and lost at least £800 each as a result.

When put into a difficult situation many people will look after themselves first. If you doubt this, ask yourself what you would do if your livelihood, family or whatever else that's important to you is threatened?

When negotiating, remember that you're dealing with a human being in front of you, not necessarily just an organisation. People are human, they're fickle and when 'push comes to shove' they'll often act in their own interests.

And maybe lose something more valuable in the process.

13 PERSONAL AGENDAS

13 PERSONAL AGENDAS

Aaron: (A passenger, speaking to Sandy, the Cabin Service Director (CSD), in the middle of a transatlantic flight.) *'Sandy, it's really not a big deal. I don't want to make a formal complaint. I was just letting you know, as it's a long flight and we're just having a general conversation, that I have not been happy with several incidents in the last year with [unnamed airline]. You did ask me, after all, so I was just being honest with you.'*

Sandy: *'I know what you're saying, but what you've told me is completely unacceptable and it reflects very badly on our airline. We need to value frequent flyers like you because, if we don't, then we don't have an airline any more. "Corporate" seem to forget that this is a people business – they treat passengers like walking money bags.'*

Aaron: *'I've tried complaining to your head office in the past, sometimes about serious things such as them changing my flight date but not offering any compensation, or a flight landing four hours late and them hiding behind "technical issues beyond our control" to avoid having to pay compensation. So, I've now given up because I've learned that it's a total waste of time. I feel I don't count and head office staff don't care one jot, even though I've been a loyal and very regular customer of theirs for more than 24 years.'*

'But it's their loss; in the last year I've diverted lots of my business to their competitors – the equivalent of at least $22,000.'

Sandy: *'And you fly every week?'*

Aaron: *'Pretty much, and a lot of it is long-haul, so your airline is now losing a lot of my business – two business-class returns to Asia from London in the last six weeks alone. It's a shame because your airline's inflight crew are universally excellent. The problem is with the faceless corporate bureaucracy at head office.'*

Sandy: *'I want you to put all of this in writing. You might have given up but I want to take on the cause for you. I've just about had enough of corporate; they don't even listen to us. As CSD, I am the most senior cabin crew on this aircraft, so if I can't get my voice heard, then who can?'*

INSIGHTS AND LEARNING

What's going on in a situation where a senior employee of a well-known service organisation is complaining more strongly about her own organisation than a regular customer who has been on the receiving end of poor service?

It's a fact of life that personal agendas vs. what's right for the business get intertwined and conflict with one another far more than is healthy or appropriate. But why is this example given rather than a more obvious one in which a person in a position of power or influence was pursuing a more insidious route to personal gain, such as taking bribes in return of awarding big contracts? This subject is discussed in case 48 - 'Corruption and Bribery'.

This example counter-intuitively illustrates how a representative from the 'other side' can strangely but genuinely align with you in a negotiation. It doesn't happen often but it can, especially if the other party is an intermediary, or a representative of the bigger corporation, who feels somewhat detached, does not agree with the approach of their superiors, or feels in some other way disengaged – as is the case with this CSD.

Have you ever been in a customer service situation when something goes wrong and the person you're talking with says something similar to the following?

- *'They've put that in since the first of the month. I don't understand why and I don't agree with it, but what can I do? They don't listen to us.'*
- *'I know what you're saying. I'd feel the same in your situation.'*
- *'To be honest, I know I'm supposed to sell you this but it's really not a good deal for you – it comes with a three year warranty anyway, so I think you're safe without it.'*

Interesting though this paradox may be, and can in fact benefit you, what can you do if you suspect someone is acting in his or her personal interests in a way that is against yours?

HOW CAN I USE THIS?

- Avoid the situation arising in the first place by establishing clear ground rules, such as insisting on those involved in business decisions declaring any known or potential conflicts of interest with the decision and themselves, or any family member or close acquaintance.
- Establish agreed criteria against which decisions will be evaluated; objective criteria act as a dispassionate, independent moral compass, against which it is difficult to argue.
- Use independent third-party evidence and advisors who have nothing to gain or lose from whichever way the decision goes.
- Insist that for any particular direction to be pursued at least two people need to support it; if there are many people involved, then a substantial majority needs to give approval.

- Ask probing questions to elicit the other person's true needs and wants; ask follow-up questions to cross-check or validate previous answers.

- When questioning the other party, observe their verbal and non-verbal reactions that may indicate responses that are less than honest.

- Ask them to argue for the opposite of what they propose; how well do they do this, if at all?

- If it is clear to you that they're not balanced in their viewpoints, they cannot see the pros and cons from all sides, or they're clearly biased, prejudiced and closed to other options, then point it out to them – negotiators refer to this as 'calling the behaviour'.

- If all else fails, challenge and expose them more directly still, stating that you believe they're taking a stance that promotes their own position and selfish ends, and refuse to negotiate further.

14 FATALISM VS. DETERMINISM

14 FATALISM VS. DETERMINISM

Randy:	(A negotiator from Northern US.) *'Abdullah, can we meet again, at 09:00 tomorrow morning to progress talks?'*
Abdullah:	(A senior manager in a company based in Riyadh, Saudi Arabia.) *'Insha'Allah.'*
Randy:	*'I'm sorry. What did you say?'*
Abdullah:	*'Insha'Allah – it means if God wills.'*
Randy:	*'Well, I'm asking you, not God. So can we meet at 9am tomorrow?'*
Abdullah:	*'Insha'Allah.'*
Randy:	*'Okay. Well, I will be here just before 09:00 tomorrow. Is it possible for us also to meet with Mr Shafiq at that time to finalise the deal?'*
Abdullah:	*'Insha'Allah.'*
Randy:	*'Look, all I'm asking is whether Mr Shafiq could be available?'*
Abdullah:	*'Mr Brown, I understand, and all I am saying is that Mr Shafiq may be available, though none of us can guarantee such things as events are in the hands of Allah. Nevertheless, I will ask him to be here, and "if it is written", then he shall be here.'*
Randy:	*'Okay. Well, let me ask you a different question. Mr Shafiq is leaving at the end of the month to take up a new position at company X. As his right-hand man, will you be taking over, will you be assuming the role of head of the procurement function?'*
Abdullah:	*'Insha'Allah.'*
Randy:	*'I appreciate that, but will you at least be applying for the vacant position?'*
Abdullah:	*'Mr Brown, there's no point in applying; it is not talked about openly, but his brother is sure to inherit the role.'*

INSIGHTS AND LEARNING

In the Middle East it can be difficult to tie people down to firm decisions or commitments, even though they're often very obliging and personable hosts.

'Insha'Allah' means 'God willing' or 'If Allah wills', and in the above example the words 'If it is written' are also used. The latter, roughly translated, means that 'if it is prophesised it is to be.'

The second question from Randy about whether the Saudi gentleman would apply for the soon-to-be-vacant position shows another cultural dimension that is prevalent in the Middle East – nepotism. It is interesting to also note that it would be almost unheard of for the incumbent's sister or daughter to get the position; it is almost always a man.

Fatalism is a belief that events are determined by fate. People who subscribe to fatalism believe they have to accept the outcome of events, and they cannot do anything that will change the outcome because events are determined by something over which they have no control – a higher power, for example.

Cultures that tend to adopt a more fatalistic view of the world include those from the Middle East, India and Pakistan. It's common in Pakistan, for example, to believe that a person's time of death is fixed and cannot be avoided. This can lead to the idea that there's little point in taking steps to avoid death because it will come at the appointed time, no matter what you do.

Fatalism can portray itself in business and negotiations by apparent apathy and/or avoidance.

In contrast, the North American culture tends to believe that it is possible to influence events or, even if outcomes and results cannot be changed, there still exists the freedom to choose how to respond, without being compelled to react in a certain way by forces beyond their control.

The meeting the next day did happen and Mr Shafiq did attend, though it did not start until 10:30 and, of course, the negotiation was interrupted periodically for prayers and accompanying ablution rituals.

HOW CAN I USE THIS?

This example has similarities to case 50 – 'When in Rome – or Athens' where you will learn what happens when a German lady and a British guy met with some Greeks. Time and timeliness are again involved, and so they do not need to be repeated here – please refer to the insights section of that case.

The added dimension in this case is one of fatalism vs. determinism.

In such cultures, if you find this hard to comprehend, understand or work with, then maybe you would be more successful working with cultures that are more similar to your own. If you have little choice, however, then you need to understand that culture runs deep, and that in some parts of the world religion and religious beliefs play a huge part in the attitudes, expectations, rituals and behaviours that we see on the surface.

If you try to fight or resist extremely strong cultural values and behaviours, then you're doomed to fail, or at least wear yourself into the ground with frustration in the process.

Assuming you do want to try to make your intercultural negotiations a success, here are some general tips:

- Taking a cultural dimension that you notice in another culture, consider in very broad terms where you think the culture 'stands' with regards to that dimension – some will be easier to identify than others, as illustrated by the examples above.

- Talk with others who have had experience of working with people from that culture and ask them which cultural dimensions they have generally found to be the most important and relevant when negotiating in that context.

- Especially talk with others who originate from that culture or who have spent time living and working within it in recent years, and who can also 'view' the culture from the perspective of your own.

- Beyond national cultures, consider, and make a few notes about, the culture of the organisation that you will be negotiating or communicating with; consult others who have had dealings with the people in the counter-party's organisation.

- Find out as much as possible about the specific person or people with whom you will be negotiating; what information do you or others already have, what is their background, their personality style and communication preferences, etc.

- Taking all of the above into account, plan your approach accordingly.

- Have 'big eyes and big ears' during your meetings and other interactions; you need to be super aware of what is going on both above and below the surface.

- Reflect on what happens and adjust your approach (if required) appropriately for the next interaction/negotiation.

- Learn and have fun in the process!

15 POWER OF LANGUAGE

15 POWER OF LANGUAGE

'Daddy, daddy, please can I stay up a bit later tonight?'

Imagine you're the father in this situation. It's a school night and normally your nine-year old daughter goes to bed earlier than at the weekend. Imagine also that, for the purpose of this exercise, she has no strong reason for wanting to stay up a bit later – she just wants to, as she doesn't feel tired. Imagine what might happen if you gave a straight 'yes' or 'no' answer to the request.

What are some of the natural consequences of you saying 'yes'?

What are some of the natural consequences of you saying 'no', and holding firm?

Don't skip ahead – put yourself in the shoes of the dad and think about a couple of realistic outcomes from each of these two polar responses – black or white, yes or no.

What if you said something else instead? What if you said 'maybe'?

Now take yourself out of this family situation. In the business world when you're negotiating or asking for something that you really want, and to which the other party does not immediately say 'yes' or 'no' but says 'maybe'…, what does that five-letter word do to you at a psychological/thinking level?

INSIGHTS AND LEARNING

'Maybe' is not a 'yes' or a 'no' – it's not black and white, it is not elation or ejection, delight or despair.

'Maybe' implies the possibility of progress and a satisfactory outcome.

If you're the person who is asking, then a 'maybe' response gives you hope that a favourable deal is possible, and you're likely to work just a bit harder to convert this into a definite yes, perhaps by making a further concession or simply by asking, *'So what would I have to do, or what would need to happen for you to say yes?'*

The dad used his 'maybe' technique on several occasions, each time managing to influence his daughter to do the things that he wanted her to do in return for acceding to her requests.

When the girl was 14 he confronted her about the messy state of her bedroom. *'Sasha, go to your room now and pick up all your clothes off the floor, hang them up or put them in the wash basket, and tidy up everything else that's lying around.'*

Sasha looked at her dad, and in a calm and controlled tone simply said, *'Maybe.'*

HOW CAN I USE THIS?

So much power from such a small word.

You can use other words, of course, to indicate the same response, such as:

- *'That might be possible, but...'*
- *'We can consider that, however,...'*
- *'I am not totally ruling it out, though...'*

In each case, by not saying 'yes' or 'no', and by keeping the metaphorical door open, you're indicating to the other party that a deal might be possible but they're going to need to work a bit harder to get it, possibly by making a bigger or earlier concession.

If you're asked, *'So what do I need to do to turn your maybe into a yes?'*, then you have what is called a buying or selling signal, i.e. the other party is willing to make a concession to tip you into the affirmative.

You can build on this indication of movement to get a little more of what you want or need, in order to clinch a deal.

One option is simply to tell them what it is that they would need to do in order for you to agree to the deal. Another is to put the ball back in their court and ask them *'So, what is it you suggest?'*

For a little more insight into these two approaches see Case 19 – 'Onus Transfer'.

16 EXPLICIT VS. IMPLICIT COMMUNICATION

16 EXPLICIT VS. IMPLICIT COMMUNICATION

This is one of the shortest cases you will read in this book. You will immediately see a connection with the case you have just read, however, the insights and lessons go further.

A Chinese participant on one of our Advanced Negotiation Skills workshops a few weeks ago, who now works as a mid-level purchasing negotiator in Denmark, and who primarily buys materials from the Chinese, told us that in her experience of growing up and working in China, 'Yes' means 'Maybe' and 'Maybe' means 'No'.

INSIGHTS AND LEARNING

Implicit communication, which the example above is attempting to illustrate, focuses on the ambiguous areas of gestures, vocal tones, actions and, sometimes, what is not said rather than what is.

People who have grown up within a culture of implicit communication know what a person from their culture means when they say certain things. For people from outside that culture the meaning of communication can be hard to interpret, or it can even be misinterpreted, leaving the recipient bemused and confused – certainly not amused!

Listener from the UK: *'But you said "yes" and now you're telling me "it's going to be difficult" – how come things have changed?'*

Implicit communication occurs more often in what are referred to as 'high-context cultures', where people leave many things unsaid. The context, made up of the environment, the situation and the parties involved, carries messages that complement the spoken word and make up for the things that are left unsaid. Indian culture is a high-context culture, as are the cultures of many Asian and Arab nations.

Explicit communication, on the other hand, deals with what a person writes or says directly. It can be very clear, sharp, direct, unambiguous and straightforward such as, *'No, I'm sorry, but I'm not going to do that.'* A person who favours or is used to more implicit communication may instead say, *'That would be difficult'*, *'Maybe'* or *'I'll try'*.

In low-context cultures, such as the US and much of Europe, where communication is more explicit, things are often spelled out more clearly and directly. To negotiators from high-context cultures, overt statements might be perceived to be a little blunt, even bordering on rude, and questions too penetrating, impertinent and direct.

There is much room for misunderstanding and frustration within negotiations and business in general if attention is not paid to this very important cultural sub-dimension of implicit vs. explicit communication style.

In a related communication sub-dimension, it's common in Nordic cultures to want to avoid conflict. This is in stark contrasts with the Dutch, for example, for whom direct and assertive communication is not only displayed, but also expected from others.

HOW CAN I USE THIS?

As with the other cultural examples within this book, awareness is half of the solution. Understanding and adaptation is the remaining half.

So, what can you do practically to further broaden your cultural awareness, understanding and effectiveness?

Whilst some of the tips below reinforce messages conveyed elsewhere in this book, by following the guidance below you are less likely to find yourself feeling like a fish out of water or committing cultural gaffs and blunders during your upcoming negotiations.

1 DEVELOP AN UNQUENCHABLE ATTITUDE OF CURIOSITY

When you see behaviour that appears unusual, meaningless or even bizarre to you, do not immediately judge or reject it. Find out why that person's acting in that way, what's behind the behaviour, and what they're trying to achieve. If you aren't curious, then it leads to disinterest, which could be perceived by others as disrespect. Also, remind yourself of how boring the world would be if we all had one global, uniform culture!

However, in negotiation situations some people do consciously behave in certain ways in order to achieve an effect or some sort of advantage. For example, pretending to get angry or deliberately playing 'poker face' to keep information and their reactions from you and to keep you guessing. These are negotiation tactics and are not related to cultural understanding.

(Contact the author if you want information on how to counter such negotiation tactics. We have amassed a collection of hundreds of tools and techniques to use to foil, disarm or push back against tactics that are used against your best interests.)

2 EXPOSE YOURSELF

At a practical level you can do this by travelling extensively, engaging with local people outside of hotels, eating in local cafés, bars and restaurants, walking the streets, taking public transport rather than taxis and getting off the 'tourist trail'.

This may feel uncomfortable at times, because you're actively pushing yourself out of your 'comfort zone'. However, this is where learning occurs, and rather than seeing it as inconvenient or uncomfortable, re-frame it as exciting or an adventure, and you're more likely to get a more genuine impression of the real culture.

3 LEARN

Before visiting a country or interacting with people from a culture different to your own read about the nation's history, heritage and traditions (which do not change), its values and behavioural norms. Talk to people who have visited, worked in or with people from that culture to learn what works and what doesn't – remembering to keep an open mind.

4 DON'T TAKE EVERYTHING AT FACE VALUE AND DON'T ASSUME

Just because the 'foreign' immigration officer speaks to you by saying, for example, *'Give me your passport'* or *'I need documents'* (without any softening pleasantries such as *'Please'* or *'Thank you'*), it does not mean she's being rude. It may just be that she has only a functional grasp of the English language and/or she works in a culture that values explicit communication.

5 CONSIDER WHETHER YOU'RE GOING TO TOLERATE OR ACCEPT DIFFERENCES

You may find yourself tolerating differences in the thinking and behaviour of others. However, that is not the same as accepting those differences. When we move to acceptance we are deepening our understanding, feeding our motivation to learn and moving more towards equality, respect and effective collaboration.

However, in some situations it can be difficult even to tolerate some behaviour, for example, people who regularly spit in the street or belch loudly after a meal. Whilst spitting in public is 'normal' behaviour in countries such as China or Turkey, in some societies it's regarded as a gruesome, disgusting, antisocial behaviour that can spread disease.

True tolerance and acceptance works both ways. Those who, for example, spit in the street in their own country should accept that when visiting countries that are significantly culturally different they should adapt their behaviour and understand why it is important to do so. They'll also avoid creating difficulties for themselves and so it is in their interest to do so.

6 LOOK FOR SIMILARITIES

It's human nature to notice things that are different, whereas things that are familiar or similar can just pass us by. If you look for ways in which you and a person from another culture are similar, aligned in your thinking, or simply share the same passion for something, then this can form the basis of resolving differences and building greater mutual understanding.

In negotiations, it could be something as simple as you both agree that you want to reach a mutually acceptable deal. By starting with that shared objective, then you will stand a better chance of achieving it as you both want the same outcome.

7 WHENEVER POSSIBLE, WORK AND NEGOTIATE FACE TO FACE

In-person, face-to-face meetings are hugely important in effective cross-cultural collaboration and in building trust between two or more parties. This is not always possible, though, with the prevalence of video conferencing, Skype and other video-based technological communication tools we can get close to it. Telephone conversations are better than email. However, without visual clues and cues, a lot of meaning and information can be lost between parties if they rely only on audio.

8 ADAPT YOUR LANGUAGE AND CONTENT

Avoid using slang, colloquialisms or expressions peculiar to your own culture, and be aware that words can mean different things to different cultures. For example (and please excuse some rather 'robust' examples in this list), 'pants', 'pissed', 'fanny pack', 'fag', 'gas', 'trunk', 'hood', 'condo', 'rubber' and 'yard' mean very different things to Americans vs. the British. It's also interesting that many of the above terms can be interpreted as being sexually explicit, rude or at least suggestive – a further source of cultural misunderstanding of meaning. If you're unaware of such subtleties then you may be taken aback by the response you get, which might even include a slap in the face!

Equally, watch out for inappropriate jokes or humour. British people have to be particularly careful not to slip into the trap of using irony (saying the exact opposite of what they really mean) as in: 'Hmmm that's an "interesting" shirt and tie combination'; using double meaning such as: 'Your proposal is outstanding'; double-entendre and innuendo, all of which are common British habits. Humour can assist in oiling the wheels of interpersonal communications, so don't eliminate it, just be extra careful when using it in cross-cultural situations.

When working with people for whom your language is not their native tongue, speak slower, user shorter sentences, rephrase if you think you're not being understood and use examples to illustrate the meaning of what you're trying to convey. Beware falling into the trap of thinking that an effective way of communicating what you want to say is to repeat the same thing again – just a lot louder!

Finally, on the subject of language, be aware that natural topics of conversation to you may be meaningless, or even a turn-off to people from other cultures. Not everyone is fanatical about football, and in Singapore talking about the weather is meaningless as it's pretty constant all year round.

9 BE FORGIVING OF OTHERS' BEHAVIOUR

In 99% of cases, people commit cultural blunders unwittingly. They do not set out to offend. Therefore, the best thing you can do in such circumstances is not to take unacceptable actions as an insult, but rather to use the occasion to educate the other person so that they don't make the same mistake twice. If roles were reversed, and you were confused in another culture, you would probably appreciate someone taking the time and trouble to tip you off about what is and what is not 'done around here'.

Don't beat yourself up if you make the occasional blunder. Learn from it, be determined not to repeat it and use your sense of humour to retain an appropriate perspective.

10 EXPLORE MULTIPLE CULTURAL DIMENSIONS

Identify those sub-dimensions of culture that are most important and relevant to the situation you face. In particular, in business and negotiation, focus on communication styles, how information is shared, different perceptions of time, the importance of relationships, power and hierarchy structures, the degree of formality and how decisions are made.

17 GOOD, CHEAP, FAST

17 GOOD, CHEAP, FAST

'The best quality carpets at the cheapest possible prices'

So proclaimed the seven-metre long red and yellow banner fluttering above the carpet warehouse.

Elsewhere in the same town a sign outside a motor repair shop says...

'We offer three types of service, good, cheap and fast; you can choose any two:

Good service cheap won't be fast.
Fast service cheap won't be good.
Good service fast won't be cheap.'

Which sign is more honest; which sign do you believe?

There is a saying in the business and negotiation world that 'some things are cheap for a reason'. Equally, some things are expensive for a reason.

Oscar Wilde more famously said, *'A cynic is a man who knows the price of everything and the value of nothing.'*

INSIGHTS AND LEARNING

If everyone bought on price, we'd all be driving around in 15-year-old beaten-up cars, cycling on stolen bicycles, walking or hitching rides at the side of the road.

PRICE DOES NOT EQUAL VALUE

Price is an objective number, the ticket price or the price you actually pay; a set number of dollars, euros, yen, etc. Value is far more subjective, and usually more important. The value of a product or service can vary wildly between those perceiving it and the situation they're in.

If you're stranded in the desert, chocolate has no value, yet you would probably give everything you have for a bottle of water, even if it were hot!

If you're flying economy/coach and at the airport you elect to pay $30 to use an airport lounge, what are you actually buying? Are you buying somewhere comfortable to sit, the 'free' food and drinks, the quiet ambience away from the hustle and hassle of the airport concourse, the 'free' magazines and newspapers, or are you buying the chance not to have to spend the next two hours mixing with the general public?

In fact, you may be buying all of these things and the value they bring is nothing to do with the price that you pay. Some would say that $30 was a price worth paying; others would rather spend it on scratch cards, a bottle of gin or both.

Also, if you don't like the price, perhaps it wasn't meant for you. If circumstances change (you have more income, your department has been given extra budget, you win the lottery, etc.), maybe you'll like the price just fine; timing, situation and context all play a part.

PEOPLE DO NOT BUY ON PRICE ALONE

Sometimes price is not even a significant factor. Many variables are involved, and in negotiation it's critical to find out which variables are most important (valuable) to the other party. Is it quality, 100% reliability (the cost of malfunction would be disastrous), image/kudos, flexibility, timing or something else?

Yes, some people have limited cash. In these cases, price is probably top of their list and, for commodities, price figures prominently; however, it's not the only thing.

SOME THINGS CAN BE TOO CHEAP

Some things are cheap for a reason. In 2013 a scandal in Europe revealed that horse meat was being labelled and sold as beef. The economics just did not add up; beef cannot be that cheap.

In contrast, for a 25 year period between 1982 – 2007, Stella Artois lager marketed itself as 'reassuringly expensive'. They have since updated their campaign slogan, but it worked for them for a quarter of a century!

Finally, some people want to buy expensive things just because other people cannot afford them… counter-intuitively they want the goods to be as expensive as possible.

HOW CAN I USE THIS?

As a negotiator, one of your jobs is to find out exactly what it is that the other party values most and, in particular, which of those things it's relatively easy for you to give, but which has a much higher value to them. Of course, you also need to think about it the other way around. What do they have that they can give to you for relatively low cost, but which has a higher intrinsic value to you?

The used-car salesperson would probably value you paying in cash today (you're going to pay anyway so what does it matter to you), and you probably place greater value on her fitting four new tyres to the vehicle (as they would cost you more in the high street than they cost her buying them in bulk as a dealer). In this way, we can find ways to make $2 + 2 = > 5$ and we make the negotiation 'pie' bigger for all to share.

If you're selling, then you need to build and emphasise the value of your proposition, and explain the benefits to the other party in ways that talk about added value and not just price.

If you're buying, then it may be that you can use price comparisons, third-party reports and independent evidence to show why the price you're being quoted is above average or unreasonable. Nowadays it is quite common for retailers, for example, to price match, so do your research and save a few shekels!

18 BREAKING DEADLOCKED NEGOTIATIONS

18 BREAKING DEADLOCKED NEGOTIATIONS

You're going to have to suspend disbelief to read this high-stakes negotiation case. Please do not read it if you're easily offended.

Our Managing Director, a more junior consultant and myself were sitting at a large negotiation table in Singapore. We were negotiating a one-year contract for the provision of consultancy services, with the potential to extend this to three years.

The Singaporeans did not like our prices and were refusing to budge. They were used to paying less than half the price we had quoted in our proposal. Our MD was most insistent that the deal was a good one and the proposal represented excellent value for money for them.

Our MD:	'Well, you will always find another provider who will claim to be able to deliver the same for a cheaper price. I can tell you from my experience that you tend to get what you pay for. If you go for a cheaper provider, then you're likely to regret it further down. the line. There is an expression… "If you buy cheap you pay twice!"'
Singaporean three-person team:	Silence
Our three-person team:	Silence
Singaporean three-person team:	Silence
Our three-person team:	Silence

Thirty absolutely excruciatingly awkward and painful seconds later the silence was broken. My more junior colleague broke it… unintentionally.

He let out an audible fart!

Two seconds later, everybody in the room erupted in laughter ☺

The Singaporeans looked at each other first, smirked and started laughing, just moments before our MD, followed by myself, and then trailed by my junior colleague – red in the face with embarrassment, release or relief – I did not know which was the greater cause of his red cheeks.

This sounds like a joke – it is not.

This really happened and what makes it sound even more like a joke is the insight and lesson learned – his unintentional interjection into the proceedings really did change the 'atmosphere' in the room!

Someone, maybe me, I forget now as we were too busy laughing, got up to open a window, which caused even more hilarity. But the main thing was that tensions had risen too high. Something had to give, someone had to do something to create a breakthrough and my colleague certainly broke through – with impeccable timing.

INSIGHTS AND LEARNING

After the incident, it took us less than 10 minutes to agree a fair deal that both sides were happy with. We compromised a bit on price, whilst the Singaporeans agreed that they did need some of the higher specification that we were recommending, and we all left happy with the solution that we shook hands on 10 minutes later.

You cannot plan events like this – sometimes the unexpected happens – and on this occasion I'm happy and relieved to say that what might sound like a totally ghastly, obnoxious and unsavoury act, in the corporate offices of a well-known international bank, really did succeed in breaking the deadlock and sealing the deal.

HOW CAN I USE THIS?

Well, do NOT spend the night before such a negotiation, stuffing your face with eggs, spinach, garlic, baked beans, lager, chillies, cabbage and Vindaloo curry!

Do learn to deal with, and to professionally break, negotiation deadlocks.

Joking aside, here are some of the things you can do:

- Change from a 'competitive' to a 'cooperative' approach; treat the deadlock as a joint problem that needs to be jointly solved – *'It's in both our interests to reach an agreement.'*
- Include a concession that's 'cheap' or easy for you to make, but more valuable to the receiver.
- Ask the other party for a concession that is cheap or easy for them, but more valuable to you.
- Propose a combination of concessions from both sides, using different variables, not just meeting in the middle on one variable.
- Ask to take a break – a few minutes, a few hours or days – to allow emotions to cool.
- Use humour; lighten up, help the other party (and yourself) to see how 'silly' this is getting, and how you may both be losing perspective and heading for a 'lose-lose'.
- Safeguard your position but offer different scenarios for reaching it, for example, introduce guarantees, alter payment terms, change the contract

wording, extend the contract, offer a volume guarantee, offer exclusivity, etc.

- Change one or more members of the team to shift the 'personality dynamic'.
- Break down the problem; deal with, and agree smaller issues one by one, to get some genuine movement and to build a sense of agreement.
- Introduce a deadline, either real or artificial, to create a sense of urgency and a 'make or break' moment.
- Introduce new information or place a different emphasis or perspective on existing issues.
- Change the risk sharing; show a willingness to share in the 'unknowns' of a deal. For example, not being sure of the 'end customer demand' can create a feeling of 'partnership' and we are all in this together, sharing the risk.
- Take a junior consultant with you to the next high-level negotiation!

19 ONUS TRANSFER

19 ONUS TRANSFER

Female diner:	'Excuse me, we're wondering how long we are going to have to wait for our food? I know we are a party of 12 and it might take longer, but there have been several other tables of guests that have arrived since us, who are now being served their main courses and we've not even had our starters.'
Waiter:	'I'm terribly sorry, madam. Let me find out what's happening and I'll come straight back to you. I know we are quite busy in the kitchen right now.'

Two minutes later…

Manager:	'Madam, I apologise for the delay. You're right, it's been more than an hour since you ordered your food and it should be coming out in a matter of minutes – in fact here it is arriving now.'
Female diner:	'Okay, thanks.'

After the meal…

Female diner:	'Excuse me, we've had a nice meal, but, as you know, it was served very late. Is there anything you can do with the bill?'
Manager:	'I guess the best I can do is to totally cancel your bill, madam.'

INSIGHTS AND LEARNING

This case shows that sometimes it's better to put the onus on to the other person/ party to suggest what they think they should do, or should be done, in order to resolve a difficulty. Or, what it is that they want you to do if you have caused a problem.

The reason for stating the latter point is that if you're the apologising party, it is important to remember that sometimes people do not want to exact massive retribution or compensation from a situation. Sometimes, a simple, humble, genuine and heartfelt apology from you is all they require.

In the above case, the diner had in her head a target of a minimum reduction of 30% off the total bill, and she would have been delighted if it had been cut in half. Knowing what we now know, if she had asked for a 50% reduction, then she would certainly have got it and would be mightily pleased as a result – and the restaurant would have at least covered its costs.

However, by asking the other party what they can do – by transferring the onus on to them – the diner got a 100% reduction. OMG! Way less than the diner was expecting or willing to pay. And, remember, that included all of the food and all of the drinks – the total bill came to more than £200 – totally written off.

The twist to this tale is that even though the diner did not pay anything to the restaurant, she did leave a large £25 cash tip to be shared amongst the kitchen and waiting staff. Let's hope they all got a portion of it and the £25 did not go straight into the manager's back pocket.

HOW CAN I USE THIS?

When faced with a tricky situation where you're unsure whether to give or demand a price, or to ask the other party for a particular concession, consider asking them first.

In negotiation circles we call this 'laying down a marker' – it's incredibly important (see Part Two).

A marker is a stated position, usually numerical, such as price or volume – it tends to be a hard number or stated requirement.

When you lay down a 'marker' you put a line in the sand, a starting point, a request, a demand or an offer. For example, a seller may say, 'We charge $1,500 per day for consultancy'; a buyer may say, 'We're looking to pay no more than €65.00 per unit.'

By so doing, they're laying down a marker – they're going first.

A good rule of thumb is to try to avoid being the first person to lay down a marker; try to get the other party to state their position first. This gives you information about the 'L' of their LIM strategy (see case 39 – 'LIM Strategy') and you can then choose how to respond.

However, there are times when you do want to state your position first, particularly if you want to 'precondition' the other party towards the beginning of the negotiation. This means that where you start the negotiation sets expectations in the minds of the other party for where you might, or might not move.

Sellers generally want to find out how much buyers are prepared to pay; they often ask about available budget. If you're a buyer, you don't need to tell them your budget. They're the vendors and they know their prices, so simply ask them to submit a fair proposal – one that stands them a fair chance of winning the business, otherwise tell them not to waste their (or your) time!

But what do you do if you need to, or want to state your position first?

- Before you even get to the marker stage do your research; what does the market or independent benchmark say about what is reasonable? Establish the zone of acceptability and then start at the top or bottom edge, or even outside of this if you're feeling bold.

- If you need to lay down a marker, and for the sake of an example let's assume the marker is a price, then aim high (seller) or low (buyer); make sure your position is stretching and realistic, as unrealistic demands make you look either out of touch or just plain stupid, and the men in white overalls will be knocking at your door!

- If and when you do move from your original position, move reluctantly, slowly and modestly; a large, early move shows you were originally way out of the ballpark and, more damagingly, that you probably still have far more to give. When you move quickly, and in a big step, you're effectively telling the other party that you were ripping them off with your first offer – don't do it.

- Avoid making a series of moves one after the other. If you've already moved several times, it implies you can, and will, move again.

- Try to get the other party to be the first to move their marker in your direction. In this way, they have moved and you have not; the gap has now narrowed in your favour and you have not given anything in return – more fool them.

- Golden rule… always insist on a concession from the other party, on another variable that is important to you, as a condition of you moving your marker – you will only move if they're prepared to move conditionally.

20 BATNA AND WALK-AWAY POWER

20 BATNA* AND WALK-AWAY POWER

Supplier X, by progressively acquiring competitors, had manoeuvred into a dominant market position, providing a key ingredient, raw material Z, to Customer Y.

Naomi: (From Supplier X.) *'Hi, Bertie. Naomi here. I'm just checking your order volume requirements for the second half of the year. We have a few months before then, but it would be good to get your anticipated future raw material Z volumes so that we can plan our production schedule.'*

Bertie: (From Customer Y.) *'Hi, Naomi. Yes, we need to talk about it but, frankly, I'm shocked by your latest price increase. In fact, the price of raw material Z seems to have been increasing way above inflation and the usual cost-drivers that we monitor, so I'm feeling very uncomfortable about agreeing to continue the contract along these terms. We order more than $15 million of raw material Z from you each year; it's a massive cost input to our business.'*

Naomi: *'I understand your position, Bertie, but the market is the market and there's not a lot we can do about that.'*

Bertie: *'Naomi, I don't buy that. You <u>are</u> the market, as you're pretty much the only supplier of raw material Z now, so you have us between a rock and a hard place!'*

Naomi: *'Well, I'll leave the question about future forecasting with you for now. We have a few months, as I say, and the oil price may fluctuate between now and then so maybe things will change.'*

Bertie: *Okay, but just so you know, because of the massive spend on raw material Z, I've established an in-house team to look at other solutions, including making it ourselves – I'll let you know in a few weeks.'*

Naomi: (Now hesitating.) *'Okay,... let me know if you need anything in the meantime. I'm sorry I cannot help you with the price.'*

Two months later, Naomi was driving to work and she noticed a newly erected sign in front of a small industrial area close to Customer Y, a site known for chemical processing. The sign said 'Site leased on behalf of Customer Y'. She was curious about this, but decided to wait to see what was happening, as it was not clear what the site had been acquired for.

---

* BATNA: Best Alternative To a Negotiated Agreement

The following week…

Bertie: 'Hi Naomi. As you know, we're looking at setting up our own pilot processing plant to produce the key raw material that you currently provide. We've realised that it's a relatively simple process, but I wondered if you would be prepared to give us a few bits of advice? We've already found a site where we can do this.'

Naomi: 'Wow, that's shocking news.'

Bertie: 'I'm not sure why. I told you a couple of months ago that your price was too high and that we were looking at bringing production of raw material Z in-house.'

Naomi: 'Yes, but I didn't think you would actually get this far, and so quickly.'

Bertie: 'Naomi, we are only at the start of the process, but you do need to know that the process of planning to bring production of raw material Z in-house has started.'

Naomi: 'Can I give you a call back tomorrow?'

Bertie: 'Sure!'

The following day Naomi called back and announced that if Customer Y were to halt their early stage raw material manufacturing process they would give an immediate 20% price reduction, from tomorrow, fixed and indexed to the oil price for the next three years at the 20% reduction.

Bertie thanked Naomi for the offer and said he would consult internally and then come back to her by the end of the week.

On Friday Bertie telephoned Naomi, accepted her offer and saved Customer Y $9,000,000 over the next three years.

The industrial unit had been taken by Customer Y on a very short lease, the billboard sign was temporary and the facility had been rented to provide extra short-term warehousing for Customer Y's finished products.

INSIGHTS AND LEARNING

This is a significant case, and one that had substantial consequences for both supplier and customer. In money alone, the impact over three years was +/- $9 million.

It also raises some questions, such as how much was the supplier abusing their near-monopolistic position, how much profit were they making, how much were they abusing the constrained position of their customer and… did the customer lie?

We are not close to the financials in this case from the supplier's perspective, but what we do know is that the supplier was able to make a massive cost reduction within 24 hours, so that would indicate a degree of prior exploitation by the supplier.

We also know that the customer needed to significantly reduce their raw material costs and, if they could not, they would have to explore other options, so they had to act, or at least be seen to be thinking about acting or preparing to act.

Did the customer lie? Maybe, maybe not – you decide.

Customer Y did lease the new site, and Bertie relied upon Naomi seeing the large sign as he knew it was on her journey to and from her office. Technically, Bertie did not lie. And in his defence, the result proved that Supplier X had been exploiting him and his company. The supplier volunteered the massive price discount, they were not forced into it, and so one might view this case as one of fair retribution.

Again, you decide.

HOW CAN I USE THIS?

BATNA is the most useful tool that, hopefully, you will never have to use.

BATNA stands for the 'Best Alternative To a Negotiated Agreement'; in other words, what is it you can and will do if you cannot reach an agreement with this party?

Having a well-developed and attractive BATNA is a great source of power in any negotiation. You can identify your BATNA in a specific situation by asking yourself the question: *'What will I do if this negotiation is not successful?'*

A key reason for entering into a negotiation is to achieve a better outcome than would be possible without negotiating.

Paradoxically, one of the greatest dangers in a negotiation is being too committed to reaching agreement, without sufficient consideration of the alternatives. You get so wrapped up in the details of the deal that you fail to take a broader perspective.

So, having a clearly thought out BATNA, or a range of alternative courses of action open to you, including the power to walk away from an unsatisfactory negotiation, gives you considerable power.

The key point is that you don't actually have to walk away, or pursue another course of action. Bertie did not in fact walk away. It's the fact that you have other options that gives you the confidence to negotiate from a stronger position. Also, if the other party knows that you have alternatives, then this can further tip the balance of power in your direction, as it did in this situation.

Attractive alternatives may not always be immediately obvious, and it may take time, creative thought and discussions with others to identify these. However, this is always time well invested, as having a strong alternative course of action, or multiple options, will significantly improve your ability to negotiate a better deal.

So, think of a negotiation or influence scenario that you're about to enter. What are your options? Can you walk away from the table? What other choices or alternative courses of action do you have, or can you create; what are the pros and cons of each?

Don't stop here; consider the BATNA of the other party… do they have one? If not, you have the power… you are in control!

21 'LOSE-LOSE' IS PERFECTLY POSSIBLE

FACELESS
ORGANISATION

21 'LOSE-LOSE' IS PERFECTLY POSSIBLE

Cameron:	(A frequent traveller, speaking on the telephone with a representative from global hotel group X.) *'Hi, yes, I was just wondering why my recent five-night stay at your hotel is not showing on my internet hotel account?'*
Hotel representative:	*'Yes, Mr Pirez, we can see the booking but, unfortunately, it does not qualify for points or credits because it was booked through an internet booking agency. As we guarantee the lowest room rates through them, we cannot also give you the points for your stay.'*
Cameron:	*'Seriously? But I stayed at your hotel for five full nights, and I specifically booked it because I was just four nights short of gaining the next loyalty membership level with your hotel group. If I had known that the stay would not have qualified, then I may have booked a different hotel.'*
Hotel representative:	*'I'm sorry to hear that, sir, but on this occasion there is nothing more I can do – the rules are the rules.'*
Cameron:	*'Well, I'm not happy. Can you please put me through to your supervisor, team leader, or someone who may be able to sort this out.'*
Hotel representative:	*'Sir, I can put you through, though I think the answer will be the same.'*
Supervisor:	*'Mr Pirez, my team member has advised me of the situation and, unfortunately, there is nothing we can do about this because we have very clear rules about awarding loyalty points.'*
Cameron:	*'Okay, I'm not going to waste either my or your time trying to fight an overly bureaucratic system. I just need you to know that I stay in about 120 hotels every year, and that by sticking to your rules, which were not clear from the start, you're potentially saying goodbye to 120 hotel nights from me for the coming year and many years to come. Are you happy with that?'*
Supervisor:	*'Sir, of course I am not happy with your decision, but there is nothing more I can do.'*

SEQUEL

Cameron did not make any more bookings with hotel group X. He placed his future bookings (worth about £20,000) between two other preferred brands. Those hotel brands benefited. Hotel group X got no more business, and hotel group X's real name has been mentioned on countless occasions by Cameron to others during his business and personal travels around the world. The hotel's brand name is not printed in this book in order to avoid any chance of litigation. The image at the start of this case study is also faceless, and it is this lack of human understanding that resulted in the company losing a valuable customer.

The lose-lose element of this story is that Cameron also lost out on the accumulated loyalty points that he had earned up until that date. However, as he stated when recounting the story, it was a price worth paying in order to 'get the b******s back' for being so short-sighted and inflexible.

INSIGHTS AND LEARNING

This is just one example of how it is possible in negotiations between supposedly well-intentioned and rational individuals for a lose-lose situation to arise.

Lose-lose outcomes can arise for a number of reasons. For example, when two parties become entrenched and refuse to budge; when one party is prepared to walk away from the deal and the other says, 'Okay, go ahead'; when one party is not bothered about getting this particular deal; or when rules and constraints mean that a deal is not possible. In all of these cases, both parties have lost valuable time and engaged in efforts with nothing to show for this other than perhaps a lesson or two.

This case also shows the power of emotion over logic. Logic would dictate that the hotel group might make an exception (not to be repeated). They would not only retain a valued customer but, as he would then be at a higher loyalty level, the company could also lock him in for even more business in the future, at the expense of their competitors. Logic also would dictate that Cameron should book with the hotel group one more time, through their official channels, and then not only gain his preferred status (with room upgrades, etc.), but also benefit from the loyalty points that he has now thrown away.

The case shows the power of one party deciding that even though forcing a lose-lose situation is going to harm them, they nevertheless continue in order to seek retribution and to harm the other party.

A more desperately upsetting example is the person who decides to commit suicide in order to 'get back' at a boyfriend or girlfriend who has jilted them. No one wins in that scenario, though it does happen.

HOW CAN I USE THIS?

If you were Cameron, you may have taken the same course of action. In fact, by giving almost all of your business to one or two hotel brands that you prefer, and which are more flexible and rewarding of your custom, rescinding a few loyalty points from another is a small price to pay.

We later heard back from Cameron that by channelling most of his business via hotel group Y, he has earned the very highest level of loyalty membership and is frequently upgraded to a suite even though he has booked the cheapest room. His view is that he took a short-term loss in order to win the prize of a much more valuable longer-term gain.

In some cases where you sense a lose-lose situation might be on the cards you can:

- Cut your losses now, avoid the conflict and walk away.
- Suggest a recess or some other temporary break in proceedings.
- Keep quiet; don't provoke things further and see how, and whether, the other party responds.
- Let other people handle it who may be in a better position to negotiate due to position, perspective or just a fresh pair or eyes.
- Bring in a mediator to help navigate a more productive middle ground between you and the other party.
- Refer to rules or to a 'higher authority' to try to diffuse or depersonalise the issues.
- Minimise the negative consequences and try to salvage the best you can from what is in any case not likely to be a positive outcome.
- Appeal to fairness or values.
- Give something in order to try to create some forward momentum, and hopefully some form of reciprocation from the other party.
- Decide that 'winning' the deal is less important than preserving the relationship.
- Reduce tension with humour.

22 'WIN-WIN' COLLABORATION

22 'WIN-WIN' COLLABORATION

Lucy's telephone rang – it was Asim, a person she had worked closely with for a three year period which ended four years ago when they both worked for a large training consultancy. Since then Lucy, and later Asim, both left the organisation to set up their own independent businesses; they had not had any contact since so Lucy was surprised and delighted to hear a friendly voice from the past.

Asim had won a new piece of business with a brand-new client in Lagos, Nigeria. He was delighted to have won the work but there were two problems. Firstly, to win the work he had put in an extremely competitive bid, which was only 50% of his normal fee rate. Secondly, the work required two trainers, and as Asim works alone he needed a training partner whom he could trust to do a great job. Lucy was top of his list.

The pair discussed who the client was, proposed dates and details of the assignment. However, after discussing the financial aspects (fees agreed with the client, expenses, some financial allowance for time lost to travel, etc.) Lucy realised that she would only cover her costs. The total revenue she would earn would be enough to cover all of her expenses and pay her a very modest day rate for the six days, i.e. she would not be out of pocket but neither would she make a profit.

After careful consideration Lucy agreed to accompany Asim on the trip to Lagos to deliver two 3-day training programmes for a total of 50 Nigerians. However, she asked if Asim could request that the client pays for them to travel business class, as the thought of travelling long distance in economy class did not sound appealing.

To cut a long story short, Asim telephoned back the next day to say that the client was not prepared to pay for business class travel for the two of them, however, he had managed to persuade them to pay for the mid-level 'Premium Economy' class.

Now, people who set up their own businesses do so for many reasons, but one of them clearly is to have a cash surplus at the end of the year. Can you list at least six reasons why Lucy might have agreed to a business deal that, on the face of it, did not leave her any better off financially? List these reasons now. Then compare your thoughts with Lucy's ten real-life responses when we asked her the same question after she safely returned from Lagos having delivered a successful job, and having gained a rather nice tan in the process.

INSIGHTS AND LEARNING

Lucy's rationale included, but was not limited to the following:

1. This was a great opportunity to work with an ex-colleague with whom I had not engaged for at least four years.

2. I had never been to Nigeria – it sounded a bit 'edgy', even frightening, but it was bound to be a great experience from a personal perspective.

3. I have no clients on the broader African continent and have never been to Africa on business, so this was a great opportunity to be able to put this on my website, to talk about the success of the project to other current and prospective clients and to reinforce the wide international nature of my work.

4. This was a great opportunity to spend six days working with several groups of Nigerians, learning from first-hand experience about their culture and ways of working.

5. My schedule was free on the planned dates and it was better to fill the diary than to stare blankly at 'empty spaces'.

6. I wanted to help out my friend and ex-colleague and this was an opportunity to re-engage and strengthen a relationship.

7. It might lead to more business from the new client. (NB: Asim and Lucy would have to be careful here – having set a precedent of low fees the client may expect the low fees to continue in future. However, that would be a new situation and a different negotiation.)

8. If I had won this work on my own, I would not wish to go to Nigeria as a lone female traveller. However, in this case, I knew I would have Asim with me so I felt okay about it.

9. The subject of the training was something that Asim was an expert on, whereas I was knowledgeable but less experienced; so this was an opportunity to strengthen my skills by preparing thoroughly and working alongside a subject matter expert and practitioner.

10. Maybe in future I will be in a similar position where I need to call upon Asim to help me with a two-person assignment, and so he'll be far more disposed to work with me if I have helped him out in the past.

HOW CAN I USE THIS?

Stephen Covey (1932–2012), a-well known authority in the area of relationships, influence and persuasion, describes win-win thinking as a frame of mind that constantly seeks mutual benefit in all human interactions – agreements or solutions that are satisfying to all involved. It's not idealistic nonsense; it can be achieved.

Many people think in terms of competitive dichotomies: strong or weak, win or lose, tough or nice. But win-win thinking centres on the paradigm that there is plenty for everybody, and that one person's success is not achieved at the expense or exclusion of another person. If we get creative, we can all win in our own way; we don't divide the pie… we work together to make the pie bigger. Win-win thinking also considers the bigger picture, relationships and the longer term.

Win-win is tough and nice, courageous and empathetic, brave and sensitive. To do that, to achieve a balance between courage to push for what you want and need, awareness and sensitivity of the context and situation you are in, and consideration for the needs of the other party, is the essence of real maturity in negotiating, in business and in life in general.

Every negotiation is different. Lucy could have refused to cooperate, stating many reasons. She could have agreed but only if certain demands were met, such as far higher fees or payment for the preparation she would inevitably need to do. She could have agreed without asking for any concessions, e.g. the flight upgrade. All of these responses would have had their own particular consequences. Lucy knows she made the right decision.

For an upcoming or current negotiation, decide how you want to operate on the courage vs. consideration spectrum; where the other party may be positioning themselves and what a good outcome would look like for both of you. Also, think through the mid to longer-term likely consequences of your chosen approach. Remember to adapt your stance according to how events unfold and, if solutions are not immediately obvious, get creative; flexibility is key to your success in achieving a 'win-win'.

Finally, try to step back from the details of a situation and ask yourself these questions:

'Overall, is this "good business?"'

Would I rather have this outcome or not?'

Even if the solution is not optimal, is it better to have it than not. If the answer is 'yes', then you should proceed and be content that you have negotiated a good and fair outcome for all.

23 GETTING THINGS INTO PERSPECTIVE

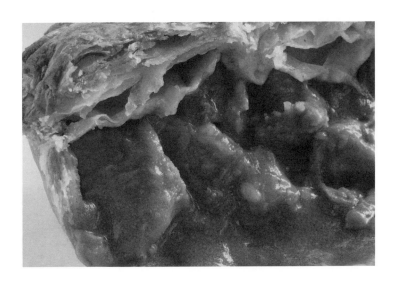

23 GETTING THINGS INTO PERSPECTIVE

Simon Goh Chan sat down with his family for dinner. They were having steak pie, bought from a supermarket. The packaging said (in Chinese) 'Filled with juicy steak chunks', and the picture on the front certainly reinforced this promise; the pie was supposed to serve at least three people.

There was one small piece of meat in the whole pie; everything else was pastry, gravy and warm air.

Simon found himself getting angry with this and threatened to take the remains of the pie, and the packaging, back to the supermarket to demand not only a refund but also something else to compensate him and his family for a disappointing meal.

It took his kids to remind him that not only was he spoiling their family meal, but the cost of the time, the MRT fare (underground rail), not to mention the stress involved, to go back to the supermarket was probably 20 times the cost of the pie.

Simon is 54, and a seasoned commercial negotiator in Asian and global markets, often negotiating deals involving hundreds of thousands of Singaporean dollars, but in this case he failed to look at the bigger picture, and he learned (again) that kids can teach supposed experts some good stuff about negotiation!

Simon was focusing more on the steak, rather than on the other far more important things that were at stake.

INSIGHTS AND LEARNING

This is about taking a broader perspective, taking a mid- to longer-term view and not allowing yourself to become angry, agitated, frustrated or irritated by the small stuff.

It is also about putting small irritations into context. Clearly, Simon was right to feel aggrieved about the situation as he felt cheated. However, if he were to stand back, as his kids did, and examine how his reaction was helping (or not), he might have decided to just put it down to a one-off piece of bad luck and forget about it.

If he was even more self-aware, he might decide to laugh about the situation and of his own reaction to it.

HOW CAN I USE THIS?

- Don't focus only on 'peanuts'; think of the bigger picture – the peanut bush or forest. In other words, don't get stuck on a trivial point or let your ego get in the way. You might win something small today, but at what cost? It may even take months or years off your life.

- Learn to laugh at yourself and some of the ridiculous or silly situations you find yourself in. If you can't find humour in a situation, life will crush you under its weight. On occasion, life's unfair and unjust. However, it's also spectacularly funny; humour balances things out if you learn to laugh at the things that really don't matter that much.

- If the issue is trivial, forget about it and move on; you stand to lose far more than you can potentially gain.

- Focus on the three or four major aspects of the deal – the ones that are really important to you – the ones that are going to make the greatest positive difference.

24 REDEFINE THE MARKET

24 REDEFINE THE MARKET

You are a senior purchasing manager for an airline. You deal specifically in the design of airline cabin interiors, the design and fitting of which you outsource to specialist providers.

You're facing a strongly distorted market with few suppliers. You're feeling squeezed on price and have few options. Most of the cabin interior design companies seem to operate along similar lines and with comparable, very high prices.

You suspect some form of cartel or unofficial collusion between your suppliers – something that you've learned is common in the airline industry, most obviously publicised by the transatlantic price rigging exposed between Virgin Atlantic and British Airways some years ago.

You need to cut costs but maintain, or preferably increase, the quality of your aircraft cabins, particularly in business and first class.

What do you do?

INSIGHTS AND LEARNING

Firstly, ask yourself what market are you dealing with? Are you operating within the aircraft interiors market?

Yes and no.

If you were to re-frame the market as one of interior design in a confined space, what does this prompt you to think of?

Could you not consider a broader market; one that includes interior designers for pleasure boats, caravans, yachts or motor vehicles?

HOW CAN I USE THIS?

You probably don't want to consider the market for the interior of space shuttles as that would totally blow your budget, but the designers of the interior of yachts or canal barges may be worth considering and approaching, or even the designers of car interiors.

No, they don't traditionally fit out aircraft, but that's the whole point. In order to achieve a breakthrough in practice we need to achieve a breakthrough in thinking, and that means not being confined by our own limited, narrow-mindedness.

Maybe a reliable, quality yacht interior designer would jump at the chance to redesign the interior of one of your older planes? The risk would be relatively small if you did it for just one plane on a pilot basis (no pun intended!), then it could provide you with a way to break out from the incumbent, expensive suppliers.

Also, with initiatives such as this you need to take a long-term perspective, so there's no need to rush into it. Planes fly for decades, so take your time, experiment, try out new unconventional suppliers on a low-risk basis and maybe you can start to lead the market with hitherto unseen innovation.

You also shape, educate, influence and expand the market. Just make sure you stay one step ahead of your competitors because good ideas are quickly copied.

25 GO EASY ON THE PEOPLE

25 GO EASY ON THE PEOPLE

Peter:	(Checking into a low-cost airline at Amsterdam's Schiphol airport.) 'Hi, Annette. I wonder if I could please just check the weight of my bag? I hope it's not over the 20kg limit, but I'm not sure as I packed in rather a hurry.'
Annette:	(Check-in assistant.) 'Sure, no problem, sir. Just pop your bag on the scales.'
Peter:	'If I need to pay an excess charge, then it's not a problem, as I know you need to stick to rules. I don't want to cause you a problem or create a fuss.'
Annette:	'Hmmm… it's a bit over. In fact, it's 21.6kg. The airline does give us permission to allow anything up to 1.0kg extra, which is at our discretion.'
Peter:	'Oh dear, sorry about that. So how much extra do I need to pay?'
Annette:	'Do you know what… I'm going to pretend it was 20.6kg, which is within my discretion, so you can put it in the hold for no extra charge – just don't tell anybody else.'
Peter:	'Wow, that's brilliant – thank you so much – I really appreciate it. Can I ask you another question though?'
Annette:	'Sure.'
Peter:	'Last week I was checking in for the same flight and a different check-in assistant made the guy in front of me pay extra, and his bag was just 20.5kg. He was in a foul mood when he arrived, and I think that only made things worse. What makes the difference between you making an exception and sticking to the rules?'
Annette:	'Sir, there is only one thing that makes the difference to me, and to most of my colleagues, and that is the approach and the attitude of the person stood in front of me at that moment in time. This 'extra discretion' will be our little secret. Enjoy your flight, sir.'

INSIGHTS AND LEARNING

Remember, whilst all 52 of these negotiation situations really happened, names and some details have been changed to protect the triumphant, the crestfallen, the innocent, the guilty, the nice, the nasty and mere bystanders.

So, Peter (not his real name) is safe in submitting this example for publication. You would have to know where Peter lives, his real name, be able to track him down to find out the real check-in assistant's name and airline and, even more disturbingly, you would have to be very small-minded to bother!

Instead, you should congratulate 'Peter' on his admirable attitude, politeness, respect for someone who has to deal with a range of difficult customers every day, and the fact that he made both himself and Annette smile that day. Isn't it great when people work together in this way, sometimes in the smallest of ways, leaving the situation in a mutually better position than they found it?

We call this a win-win, or at least a small victory for human decency and respect for the individual on the other side of the 'table' (check-in desk).

HOW CAN I USE THIS?

In negotiation circles, the importance of being hard and firm on the 'issues', but respectful and gentle with the 'people', is often emphasised.

Yes, you will meet some a*******s in your business and personal life, and some negotiators are so intolerable and unreasonable they should be taken out and shot (you will find a few examples of such people within this book if you need further convincing). However, most people don't come to work each morning thinking, 'What can I do to totally screw up someone's day?'

There is a well-known and well-accepted expression in influence and communication circles… 'Behaviour breeds behaviour'. What goes around comes around, and you often respond in a similar way to how you are yourself treated.

These two-minute interactions at the same airport check-in desk in Amsterdam beautifully illustrate how one person approached with the wrong attitude and had to pay an extra €25 for an extra 500g, and the other, with a more considerate attitude, paid nothing for an extra 1.6kg.

There is another classic negotiation mantra… 'Be firm on the issues but go easy on the people' – hence, the title of this case.

Most people are 'human' beings – treat them as such, and not only are you likely to come out with a better result negotiation-wise, you're also more likely to be able to sleep at night. You might even make a new friend!

26 PEOPLE LIE

26 PEOPLE LIE

Fabia was stuck. Stuck with using hundreds of thousands of a supplier's component that had a long patent on it, and so she was unable to go to other, cheaper, generic suppliers to ask them to make something the same or similar.

Her frustration was compounded because she knew that the cost price of the component was a tiny fraction of what she was being charged by the supplier. She likened it to being trapped into buying original manufacturer's ink cartridges for printers when she knew that there were other generic 'copy' cartridges on the market for just 15% of the price.

One day she decided to type the patent number into Google in order to check when the patent was due to expire.

Fabia was disappointed to see that the patent still had many years to run – another six. So unless she could find some other way out of this situation she was trapped and compelled to keep on using this low-value but very highly-priced component.

However, Fabia's disappointment soon turned to delight when she realised that the patent number was for a completely different product. The product she had been buying was now out of patent protection.

That afternoon, after challenging the supplier on this point and receiving a somewhat reluctant admission that, yes, the patent had indeed expired, and that they could not explain why the wrong patent number had been printed on the components, Fabia invited competitive bids from three other providers.

In addition to saving her company upwards of €100,000, Fabia learned several lessons in the process.

INSIGHTS AND LEARNING

Don't take everything you read or are told at face value.

Check out small details, especially when there is a lot at stake or the contract value or material cost is relatively high.

Challenge your suppliers and get them to substantiate their claims.

HOW CAN I USE THIS?

If you work in commercial purchasing, do not accept that you know the market until you have:

- Used an online sourcing directory, preferably with global coverage.
- Referred to a specialist trade directory for the category of interest.
- Networked with peers in the same industry in other countries.
- Attended trade fairs or exhibitions in another country.
- Commissioned a third-party market review by a specialist agency.
- Engaged a sourcing agent to locate suppliers in low-cost countries.
- Done some internet searching for alternative products/services.

However, a word of warning in relation to the last point. Do not overly rely on internet search engines; they're not effective sourcing tools on their own. Data is filtered by others, paid for by commercial organisations to appear at the top of the page or in side bars, and is of variable quality or even downright wrong. Internet search engines are an obvious place to start, but they'll not necessarily provide you with the optimum solution.

27 RECIPROCITY

27 RECIPROCITY

Alastair was waiting patiently in the queue to pick up the van that he had rented for the day. It was 08:30 and the busiest time of the day for the rental company.

The woman at the front of the queue was distressed as she was apologising for returning a damaged vehicle. The next person in line, having returned his vehicle, had no way of getting back home, and the lady behind him and in front of Alastair, was waiting to see if she could hire a van on the spot – without having booked in advance.

Alastair was then heartened to hear the distressed woman offer the man with no car to get home a lift with her – a distance of five miles in the opposite direction. It made such a positive impression on Alastair that as the two strangers were leaving the shop he announced to everyone, including those behind him in the queue, that he thought it was an admirable act of kindness. Everyone smiled. It seemed that human kindness, even between strangers, still pervades when people find themselves in difficult or stressful situations.

Then the young lady in front of Alastair stepped up to the desk. She was distressed to learn that no vehicles were available that day as they had all been booked in advance. The lady seemed anxious to know what to do – asking if she could take the damaged vehicle ('Sorry, no', was the reply, as it was no longer roadworthy) and asking if they had any more branches or access to vehicles from other vehicle hire agencies, etc. She clearly needed a van that day otherwise her plans would fall apart.

Alastair stepped forward.

Alastair:	'Excuse me, how big a van do you need and for how long?'
Lady:	'Err… I'm doing a favour for an elderly neighbour. I've helped her do a big clear-out of her house, all the rubbish is sitting in her front garden and the neighbours want it all moved today.'
Alastair:	'So you need a mid-sized van for half a day?'
Lady:	'Yes – but there are none available.'
Alastair:	'Well, I have the same requirement. I have a mid-sized van booked for the whole day, but I only need it for the morning. Would you like to take my van for the afternoon? I have no need for it after 1pm.'
Lady:	'Really? Is that a possibility?'
Alastair:	'I don't see why not. We would have to clear it with the guy behind the desk, but there's got to be a solution to this that keeps everyone happy.'

What followed was some negotiation between Alastair, the young lady and the guy behind the desk. After some initial hesitancy, the booking clerk realised that what was being proposed was actually a very sensible and pragmatic solution. His difficulty lay in the fact that it was not in-line with company policy.

Details aside, they found a way to make it happen.

A key point in this story is that Alastair was willing to gift the van to the lady for the afternoon and did not expect anything in return. After all, he had no need for the van after 1pm so it would just be sitting idle; it would be a wasted resource, much needed by someone else.

However, the lady was absolutely insistent that she pay half of the day's rental, and would not take any refusal from Alastair to accept her money.

INSIGHTS AND LEARNING

Acts of random kindness can have a positive effect on those who witness them, and can encourage them to carry out similar goodwill gestures.

Witnessing the willingness of the first woman to give an unknown man a lift home inspired Alastair.

He, in turn, was keen to help out a lady in distress.

The booking clerk, having witnessed both events, felt moved to 'break the rules', make a three-way agreement and, so long as both Alastair and the lady signed a hastily improvised piece of paper to protect the clerk in case anything went wrong, he was prepared to turn a blind eye and allow the technically improper arrangement. Yes, technically improper, but at least it was between 'consenting adults'!

Behaviour can breed reciprocal behaviour from the other party/parties.

This story also demonstrates the power of 'reciprocity' in human exchange and negotiations.

HOW CAN I USE THIS?

Most people feel an overwhelming urge to repay debts, to do something in return when something is done for them – a favour, a kindness or an unexpected gift. You know this is right; you feel it yourself.

Psychologists and sociologists assert that the urge to reciprocate is a universal principle that transcends cultures. It means that we're all bound, even driven, to repay debts of all kinds. When someone has done something meaningful for us in the past, and they ask for a favour later, we often quickly and automatically say

'Yes', because subconsciously we know we're indebted to them, and we need the psychological release to be able to feel that the 'books are balanced'.

This incident is an example of human kindness with no expectation of anything in return. However, in the harder field of commercial negotiations it's wise not to feel too indebted to another person; it can lead to a disempowering and weak position from which to negotiate. If you're smart, you will make the law of reciprocity work *for* you.

1 GIVE SOMETHING AWAY FOR FREE

This could be a gift, a service, information, assistance, a compliment or anything in which the other party finds value. Try to give something away that doesn't cost you much, but which has high value to the other party (as in our case study above). Later, if you're in a position to ask for something, then the feeling of indebtedness that the other person feels should come into play. However, there is no guarantee that reciprocity will kick in, and neither should something be deliberately given away in order to manipulate the other party to reciprocate unless you're doing it as part of a mutually agreed concession, in which case this is a fair 'trade'.

2 BE THE FIRST TO GIVE SOMETHING

The person who gives first is in control and holds a moral position. It is often said that it is better to give than to receive. Who wants to be the person in the group who is renowned for never buying the first round of drinks at the bar, or waiting until the end when the bar closes and so they don't get to put their hand in their pocket? I knew someone who did put their hand in their pocket at the end of the evening, but it was just to assure themselves that all the money they brought out that night was still unspent!

Most people are reasonable, and neither are they fools, so a lack of reciprocity quickly shows through. So, whilst you should not hold people to the fire for a lack of reciprocity, you could point out how you helped them in the past, and so you would hope that they could reciprocate on this occasion.

3 MAKE IT PERSONAL

Be clear that it's coming from you, not from some faceless organisation; people do favours and 'paybacks' for other people, rarely for inhuman organisations.

4 SURPRISE THEM

For example, offer something the other party did not ask for, go the 'extra mile' or offer to do another favour or kindness a few weeks later.

On balance, in life in general, beyond the field of negotiations, the more you give the more you will receive. Often this relates to different things, at different times and from different people. Another commonly quoted expression, mentioned in case 25 - 'Go Easy on the People', is 'What goes around comes around' — sometimes in a totally different form, at a different time and from a different direction.

Even if it doesn't work every time, isn't it better to give than to receive? Isn't it better to be able to sleep at night?

28 HOLDING YOUR GROUND

28 HOLDING YOUR GROUND

Peter got a call out of the blue.

It was from a project management agency he'd never heard of. They had discovered him via the internet and were enquiring as to whether he could be available to run a short project, just one week, for one of their clients – in the Caribbean!

Peter was in relatively high demand in his home country, and occasionally in mainland Europe, but the thought of taking a paid-for business trip to work for a new client in the Caribbean was extremely attractive. Thankfully, the initial approach was not via a video call because he could not stop himself grinning from ear to ear.

However, rather than jump at the assignment, Peter tried his best, and actually succeeded, in not appearing overly keen, too available or too cheap. He composed himself and responded calmly and professionally.

Peter did this by asking lots of questions rather than trying to persuade the intermediary party why he was the person for the job. He resisted sounding excessively keen, he pointed out that his diary was quite busy and so they would have to plan carefully if he were to find time to fulfil the assignment and he said, quite openly, that they would need to discuss fees early in the negotiation, so as not to waste each other's time.

Peter was a bold man, some might say foolish, in that he was taking a big risk by playing it so cool. Others might have just snapped the agency's hand off and agreed to do it for any price. However, Peter knew his value. He knew he was in a relatively strong position because they had approached him and he already had a healthy pipeline of work.

Peter also knew that intermediary agencies like this were used to paying rather low fees to their sub-contractors, whilst charging the end client at least twice that rate.

So, in addition to playing it cool, Peter also decided to go in high with his fee rate.

Peter:	'Okay, it's possible that I can do this for your client, however, it would need to be on dates when I am available for a full week, and the fees would need to match the value I can bring.'
Agency:	'Yes, dates are flexible. What do you normally charge for work like this?'
Peter:	'My day rate is X.'

Agency:	'Oh dear. That's going to be a problem. For work like this we normally pay our associates Z.'
Peter:	'Yes, you're right. The gap between us is too wide; you seem to be paying just a third of what I normally charge. I don't think on this occasion we're going to be able to find a way to make this work. That's a shame. I hope you have others you can call upon to fulfil the assignment.'
Agency:	'Well,... we do have other people but maybe not with your specific expertise.'
Peter:	'Okay. It seems that you want me to work through you to meet your client's needs, but you're not used to paying fees at this level. I will tell you what I am prepared to do, on this occasion alone. If you're able to negotiate a higher rate between you and your client – a rate that would mean that you pay me a guaranteed day rate of Y, which is two-thirds of my normal day rate, then I will agree to that. However, I cannot go any lower than Y so if you can negotiate a higher rate with your end client, justified by the specialist nature of the work and my expertise, then I am happy to sign a contract for the six days. What do you think?'
Agency:	'Peter, I'm doubtful the client will pay, but I will see what I can do.'
Peter:	'Okay, and thanks for contacting me. Please come back to me if you get a positive response from your client. I can promise you one thing – the results I will get for them will be exceptional – you only have to ask my other clients if you need evidence of that. I assume you've seen the testimonials on my website.'

INSIGHTS AND LEARNING

The next day Peter's phone rang and he was awarded the contract at Y per day.

Peter never found out how much the end client paid for his services, as such things are not discussed when intermediaries are involved. It's a professional code within the industry. Of course, he hopes and expects that the intermediary also made a profit by being able to negotiate upwards their fees for the assignment, or maybe they decided to take a financial hit on this one deal in order to keep their long-term client happy – Peter still does not know to this day.

What the agency did not know was that Peter's target day rate was Y, the rate he ultimately achieved, and that he was using X as a high-level 'anchor' to set expectations in the mind of the intermediary. This is sometimes called 'pre-conditioning' (see Part Two).

Peter would probably, if pushed, have agreed to do it for just Z per day, but then he would have had to lose face and concede further as he had already told the agent that Y was his 'walk-away' price. Remember, he really wanted to do this job, so if he were pushed, he would probably have conceded, and reluctantly agreed to Z, so as not to lose what sounded like a fantastic opportunity.

So, even though Peter did secure the deal, and by the way he did a fantastic job, he took the risk of losing the whole six-day contract, and a trip to the Caribbean, by holding out. Or did he? What do you think? What would you have done in Peter's circumstances?

Peter privately knew he was pushing for a high day rate, but he also knew that agreeing to a lower day rate, if the deal really was being taken off the table, and losing a bit of face in the process in order to secure the assignment, was something he was prepared to do. Saving face vs. saving fees – one of negotiation's fine balances!

Peter was determined to go to the Caribbean – he was just careful not to let the agency suspect this, and on this occasion it worked.

Like all negotiation game play, however, there are no guarantees, and on other occasions this tactic has not paid off, neither for Peter nor for others in a similar situation. This is just one reason why negotiations are so fascinating.

HOW CAN I USE THIS?

One of the most powerful tactics you can use in a negotiation is to threaten to walk away from the deal, or indicate that you're close to doing so. You don't actually have to walk away, you simply imply that you're getting close to it or you will walk away if necessary.

However, it's a dangerous game to play unless you have a BATNA – a 'Best Alternative To a Negotiated Agreement' (see case 22 and Part Two for more information). If the other party calls your bluff and you do not have a BATNA, or you're not genuinely prepared to walk away, then you may quickly find yourself in a lose-lose situation.

If A makes an offer to B, then B could simply say they already have a better offer from C. It's not necessary for B to say exactly what the better offer is, or even to name C, in order to keep A guessing. B could even quote something that is better than C's offer if B chose to lie.

The problem for A is that if they call B's bluff, and B really does have a better offer, then A loses the deal and B agrees a contract with C. Both B and C win.

A problem arises for B if they do not have a BATNA, and they're then stuck with nowhere to go, or they have to lose face by continuing to negotiate. But, hey, B can't complain… he/she caused the problem by lying!

Threatening to walk away, but not actually doing so, can be a useful way of testing the boundaries of what is possible and how far the other party is prepared to move. It might flush out a 'final offer', for example.

But what can you do if you're in the negotiation and the other party indicates they're going to walk away?

- Have your own BATNA – in fact, you should never enter into a negotiation unless you have an alternative or are able to walk away yourself; having a BATNA gives you a great deal of negotiating power.

- Know as much as possible about the other party; how desperate are they to achieve a deal? What alternative options do you think they have/might have?

- Call their bluff, but keep the door open; say, *'Okay, it's a shame we're not able to agree terms; please give me a call if things change.'*

- If you think they're genuinely about to walk away, could you accept these terms? Is it still good business? Is it better to take it than to leave it? This key negotiation philosophy of a deal still being 'good business', and better to have something rather than nothing, was previously mentioned in case 22 – 'Win-Win Collaboration'.

- If you really do want this deal, then ask, *'How much better do I have to do?'* However, beware that whilst this question can flush out a resolution and achieve closure, it is a question that indicates that you, and they, know you're coming from a weaker position. This aspect has also been referred to earlier in case 19 – Onus Transfer.

- Can you accept their position, but at the same time negotiate more favourable terms in relation to another variable that's important to you? In other words, can you trade variables?

29 TOO EXPENSIVE

29 TOO EXPENSIVE

Whilst an extremely short case, this nevertheless contains a potent message.

William: (Potential car buying customer.) *'Thanks Nina, I appreciate you've spent a lot of time with us in the last few days, looking at the car we're interested in, and trying to find a configuration that suits our budget. However, my wife and I have spoken about it overnight and we've come to the conclusion that it's just too expensive – sorry.'*

Nina: (Car dealership salesperson.) *'When?'*

INSIGHTS AND LEARNING

What on Earth do you think of Nina's response? Was she not listening? Has she been drinking? It seems to be totally out of context and surreal. It does not appear to be related to, or in answer to, William's statement.

Why would Nina answer with the one-word question, *'When?'*

Timing, time, urgency, chronology and the sequence and phasing of events are incredibly important aspects of negotiation.

What Nina was referring to was one of the sub-dimensions of time, the concept of the 'time value of money'.

Money today is not worth the same as money tomorrow or rather, more significantly, the value of money in six, 12 or 24 months from now. It is also not worth the same as it was five years ago. Inflation and, at the time of writing (2015), in the UK, stagnation or even deflation, influence the 'moment-in-time' value of money.

The concept of introducing the variable of staged payments, a deposit followed by monthly instalments or some other form of loan is as old as time itself. However, what Nina cleverly did with her one-word question was to startle the couple, and to make them seriously consider whether they *could* afford the car – just over a longer time frame.

This case is not about the blindingly obvious strategy of suggesting a loan. It's about the change in thinking and circumstances that can be achieved in a negotiation if you surprise the other party by doing or saying something unusual – something they do not expect.

Such events create a discontinuity; they can change thinking, the direction of the negotiation, they can create decision points and the ultimate outcome.

Another example of saying something unexpected again involved a car salesperson, who would often say to a prospective customer, *'You're right. I think this is too expensive for you. Perhaps you should consider a model a bit further down the range; something that's more affordable.'*

It did not always work, but in more than 50% of cases the salesperson claimed that the prospect would protest, saying that in fact they were interested in the higher specification vehicle and that, despite what they may have said previously, they could afford it.

You can work out for yourself the logical sequence of events from that point forward!

HOW CAN I USE THIS?

One of the principles of effective negotiation is to never become too predictable.

When you become predictable then the other party is pretty sure how you're going to react in any given situation; they can plan for it and act accordingly. You make it easy for them to play, and to win the game.

However, when you do something that's unusual, out of character, surprising or even shocking, it changes the game.

In the above examples the element of challenge and surprise helped to move things forwards and, in fact, by all accounts, the car purchasers were very happy with the deal and their new vehicles. We might argue that the first example was helpfully clever, whereas the second was cleverly manipulative, but whatever your view, take the lesson from this that occasionally doing or saying something unusual or unexpected can achieve movement, it can achieve a breakthrough in a negotiation.

Think about whether and how you might have settled into predictable negotiation approaches, style, strategy or tactics, and how you might shake things up a little next time around; particularly with long-standing relationships where the other parties have got to know you very well.

Surprise them – but in a nice way!

The concept and sub-dimensions of time are so important in negotiations that we have included a few more cases on this (see case 8 – 'Threat of Substitution').

30 DON'T DROP YOUR GUARD

30 DON'T DROP YOUR GUARD

The Managing Director and Key Account Manager of a small manufacturing company were meeting with the lead purchaser at a well-know, mid-sized retail organisation.

The retailer was a new prospect to the manufacturer and the suppliers were excited at the prospect of winning the retailer as a new, high-profile customer. If successfully agreed, the deal would mean the retailer would become one of their largest customers.

The meeting went well and at the end they agreed terms in principle, including all of the key variables such as projected volumes, pricing, quality, delivery schedules, payment terms, etc. A contract would be drawn up by the suppliers in the next couple of days and would be signed by the purchaser and returned within three working days of receipt.

The office block had a large car park and as the two visitors walked to the MD's 7-series BMW they excitedly reviewed the meeting. As they got to the car, just before they walked to the driver and front passenger doors they did a flamboyant, spontaneous 'high-five' to celebrate their mutual success.

As they opened the car doors, they both glanced back up at the building for one last look.

The lead purchaser was standing watching them from the window – arms crossed.

The next day they received an email from the lead purchaser announcing, with regret, that he would not be agreeing the contract after all. He said that he could not go into details as to why, quoting 'internal reasons', but he wished them well in their future endeavours.

INSIGHTS AND LEARNING

Why do you think the contract was cancelled before it had even been written?

The MD and Account Manager never found out the reason(s), but they had their suspicions. The event haunts them to this day considering the amount of potential revenue they lost. In 24 hours they went from elation to deflation, from a financial situation at their manufacturing plant that was okay but slipping, to one that now threatened the survival of their factory.

The positive side of this story is that the factory did survive, and is still trading today – seven years later.

The educational value of this story is to ponder why the contract was pulled.

Could it be that the purchaser did simply change his mind? Could it be that something internally had changed within just 24 hours, which meant that he regrettably was unable to commit after all? Could it have been something else that is totally understandable from a business perspective?

Or, could it be that seeing the self-congratulatory behaviour in the car park left the purchaser with the impression that he had been screwed? Could he have resented the fact that they were climbing into a 7-Series BMW?

Neither we nor the manufacturers will ever know. What the frustrated suppliers do know is that the deal they had agreed with the retailer was a fair and reasonable one. They did not come away thinking they had won at the retailer's expense, they were just happy and excited at securing a deal with a big new customer.

HOW CAN I USE THIS?

This painful tale has a very obvious lesson. However, for absolute clarity, here are some specific tips:

- Please remember to keep your celebrations private; hold off until you're well away from the scene of the negotiation.

- Don't brag about your negotiations, or at least only do so privately to people who are on your team, on your side and who can be absolutely trusted.

- Think about how you would feel and react if, for some reason (albeit without any specific proof), you suspected that you had been screwed by the other party.

- Remember that perception and reality can be very different; the reality of celebrating a fair deal, which was more about the relief of securing a new, big customer, can be very different from the perception from the upper floor window of: 'Those guys have screwed me – I don't know how or why, but I am not going to be treated like this.'

- Think about how appropriate it might be, regardless of your position, to turn up to negotiate with another party in a very expensive, luxurious 'status' car. If you must, then perhaps you should park it around the corner, or perhaps you should let your logical brain take control of your inflated ego!

31 DON'T ASSUME TOO SOON

31 DON'T ASSUME TOO SOON

Isabelle was telephoned out of the blue. It was a head-hunter acting on behalf of Company Z, a direct competitor to her current employer – so it was a sensitive situation.

Isabelle was interested enough to have an initial conversation, and she then went to meet the recruiter for a face-to-face meeting in a local town in the Netherlands.

Over the next eight weeks Isabelle was drawn further into the recruitment process, which included Company Z flying her to Paris on three occasions to meet the recruiting manager, along with a team of other senior people to whom she was required to give a 15-minute presentation followed by questions, and to meet once more with her hiring manager.

On the third trip to Paris Isabelle brought her husband, having left her two small children at home with her mother. They were accommodated for the whole weekend in a nice hotel, with all expenses paid by Company Z, and they were helped with information about relocating to and living in the city, advice about accommodation, schools and other practicalities.

Isabelle and her husband were very excited to be told on their return to the Netherlands that all was in order and that Company Z was drawing up a contract for her employment. The final stage was that Isabelle was to travel out to Paris just one more time, on a day trip, to meet the Chief Executive Officer in order to 'shake hands and seal the deal.'

Isabelle and her husband now told their children about what was soon to be happening, to prepare them for what would be a significant life change for all of them. The kids were curious, a bit apprehensive, but at the same time excited. They started drawing pictures of Paris and the Eiffel Tower and stuck them on their bedroom walls.

The following Friday Isabelle caught the early morning flight to Paris, met with the CEO for about 15 minutes, and was then left waiting for more than an hour before she could meet, for the final time, with her hiring manager. The hiring manager was in a meeting with the CEO.

When he emerged Isabelle asked what needed to happen now and, in particular, if they had the contract for her to sign before she left for the airport.

The contract wasn't ready, so the hiring manager said that he would arrange for the contract to be emailed to her first thing on Monday morning.

On Tuesday morning the recruiter telephoned Isabelle to inform her that

Company Z would not be making an offer after all. No explanation was ever offered. It later transpired that the hiring manager had left Company Z.

INSIGHTS AND LEARNING

Imagine the amount of investment from Isabelle, her husband and, latterly, her young family in this process.

Time committed, anticipation, thinking time (often all-consuming), time off work from her current employer, having to make excuses to them as to why Isabelle needed to have 'occasional' days off, the opportunity cost of using up five trips for interviews vs. what else she could have done with that time. The sheer emotional energy involved in such a life decision, personal research into location, company, neighbourhood, housing, schools, culture, what you do with your current house…etc. It consumed them for the best part of six weeks. Then the kids got involved, they became curious, excited at the prospect, and then expectant of an adventurous move to a fabulous European city.

What about the investment from Company Z?

The hiring manager's time, four senior managers attending the presentation and staying for the group interview, administration of all of the trips (flights, transport and hotels), cost of the flights, hotels and transfers, time of the CEO. What about the lost opportunity from who else they could have hired during this time, having to start all over again, recruiter's fees to get the candidate to the final stage (not insubstantial and probably dwarfing all of the other costs), loss of face from the hiring manager…, etc.

This is a classic 'lose-lose' situation.

WHY DID IT HAPPEN?

Isabelle was distraught to hear the decision, via mobile phone, whilst she was conducting a performance review with one of her direct reports.

Yes, one should never answer a call in the middle of someone else's performance review, but remember this is a real-life case, this is what really happened and Isabelle was desperately keen to hear of the final job confirmation. So, when she saw the recruiter's name flash on her mobile phone screen she simply had to take it and excused herself for a couple of minutes.

Imagine how hard it was for Isabelle, on hearing the news, to then continue to conduct the performance review with her direct report.

This was a lose-lose-lose situation. Nobody won over this six-week period.

So, back to the question above… why did Isabelle not get the job?

As no clear explanation was given, this can only be open to speculation. However, Isabelle did admit that what was supposed to be a handshake formality with the CEO actually turned into more of an interview. That did not faze her, as Isabelle had come so far, she's a competent professional and she felt that she handled his questions well.

However, and what might have been more significant, Isabelle also revealed that she did not warm to the CEO, and she felt that for some reason he seemed to take a dislike to her. The chemistry was wrong and she was left feeling that something was not right.

Speculation, yes, but as with some of the other cases in this book, form your own opinion and consider why a situation could have got so far, with lots of tangible and intangible costs and investments on both sides, only for it to fall over at the last hurdle.

HOW CAN I USE THIS?

The lesson from this case is not so much about how a lose-lose situation can arise – as Isabelle is still not clear to this day about exactly what went wrong. The lesson is about not 'counting your chickens too soon', i.e. not before the eggs have hatched and the chicks look healthy and well.

We have all been in situations where we think we've reached a deal or are almost certain to have it in the bag, barring just receiving the paperwork. A common example is when buying or selling a house and at the last moment the buyers or sellers renege on the deal – very frustrating and very costly.

The message here is simple. If you're a seller, you can only be sure the sale has been made when the money hits your bank account. When you're a buyer, you can never be sure the deal meets your requirements until the product has arrived or the service has been delivered and everything conforms to specification.

Get things in writing, get the details clarified and documented, follow due diligence

---

* Isabelle and her family quickly got over their initial disappointment. Looking back, 10 years later, she's wholly confident that the move would have been a mistake.
Her career in the subsequent 10 years took a direction that she could not have anticipated and is mightily happy with.
She, her husband, and two teenagers are now living happily in Vancouver, Canada – by many accounts, one of the best places in the world to live.

and… something else – trust your intuition and gut feel. Isabelle left Paris knowing that something was not right, but could not quite put her finger on it. Three days later her intuition proved correct.

32 POWER PLAY

32 POWER PLAY

Olga:	(A client, speaking to a supplier over dinner in a restaurant – in a raised tone of voice.) *'Giselle, I'm not happy. You're resisting progressing this project and, frankly, I'm getting p****d off with you dragging your feet.'*
Giselle:	*'Olga, you think I'm dragging my feet; the reality is I don't agree with what you're trying to do, and you're pushing this initiative through the organisation far too fast; it's bound to meet resistance. I think it's set up to fail; that's why I'm resisting.'*
Olga:	(Now shouting and pointing aggressively at Giselle.) *'Right… I've just about had it with you… don't forget who the customer is in this situation, I pay your bills, so you either do it or you don't do it, take it or leave it – what's it to be?'*
Giselle:	(Remaining calm and unruffled on the outside but feeling emotional internally.) *'Okay, Olga. Firstly, thanks for giving me the choice. On this occasion I will leave it.'*
Olga:	(Now standing up and shouting even louder.) *'If you refuse, then that's it. You can forget about any work from me going forwards.'*
Giselle:	(Still remaining calm.) *'Olga, you just gave me the choice, and I made my choice. Anyway, I think you're right… we've worked together for about five years and so it's probably time to say our goodbyes and move on. It's a shame about all of the other projects because you're now going to have to find someone else to do those for you as well.'*
Olga:	(Now sitting down and calming down.) *'Look, this is stupid. You know I can't find someone else at the drop of a hat to take on all the things you're doing for me.'*
Giselle:	*'Yes, I know, and I am prepared to help. We just need to find a way to do this project with a slightly different approach and slower implementation.'*
Olga:	(Now much calmer.) *'So what do you propose?'*

INSIGHTS AND LEARNING

This was a big risk situation – a huge risk for both parties – and one that almost ended in a dramatic 'lose-lose'.

Firstly, it shows what can happen when people let emotions get the better of them. Secondly, it shows that threat and intimidation can be potent negotiation weapons. Thirdly, however, and the main lesson from this tense situation, is that power, the abuse of power, or the assumption that one party is in a much more powerful position than the other, can backfire.

Yes, Giselle stood to lose a lot of work. However, what she also knew was that the client needed her more than she needed the client. Hence, why she felt able to calmly stand her ground and refuse to buckle under pressure. In addition to being a strong lady, Giselle is a professional consultant, and so her experience and professional values told her that the nature and approach of the project were ill-founded. After all, why would a client employ a consultant and then not take their advice?

Giselle took a risk, but the client took a bigger one, and once she realised the hole she had dug for herself she came to her senses.

The story ends positively. This robust exchange of views, and the fact that Giselle stood up for herself and for what she thought was right, actually further cemented the client/consultant relationship and they went on to work together closely for many years.

HOW CAN I USE THIS?

When negotiations get personal and/or emotional then a warning bell is sounding.

Consider examples from your own professional and personal life when a situation had escalated into shouting, finger-pointing, personal attack, accusations, insults or even just an exchange of sarcastic comments; the outcome is rarely good.

When emotions and egos become entangled with the 'problem' in negotiations it adversely affects your ability to see the other party's position, interests and needs clearly. This results in adversarial rather than cooperative interactions.

Professional, principled negotiators make a clear distinction between jointly and rigorously tackling problems and avoiding attacking the people involved. People are human beings. Sometimes we need to remember that the relationship and what we stand to gain or lose from a personal level is often far more important than a knotty business problem that we are facing today.

Keep these steps in mind if you anticipate a difficult negotiation:

- Clarify perceptions from both sides.
- Put yourself in their shoes – genuinely.
- Recognise that emotions are involved and, in some cases, these are understandable.

- Remember, experience has taught us that when heightened emotions are involved people may say and do things that they later regret – so try to remain as objective as possible and, if nothing else, slow down, pause, think and then act with more insight and intelligence.

- Communicate rationally and clearly; stick to the facts and remain objective. In the words of Stephen Covey, *'Listen first to understand, then speak to be understood.'*

- Do not allow the other party to 'hook you' into an emotional reaction. If they get emotional, then let them 'blow off steam' without interrupting, getting emotional yourself or taking it personally.

- Remember, when a person gets emotional it usually means that they're losing control – neither be the person to lose your own sense of control nor to be controlled.

- Try to understand the problem that lies behind the emotional response from either the other party or, indeed, yourself.

- Present proposals in terms of mutual, shared interests; aim to get back to, or as close to, a 'win-win' situation as possible.

- Make sure that all parties participate in the process of issue resolution.

- Remember to tackle the problem; do not attack the people.

33 BLUFF

33 BLUFF

Ron: (Sales representative, speaking with his boss.) *'Ivan, can we talk about my salary?'*

Ivan: *'Err, okay. What's the matter?'*

Ron: *'Well, to come straight to the point, I think I'm worth more than what you're paying me.'*

Ivan: *'Ron, we've had this conversation in the past. You know that budgets are tight, and when you've raised this previously you've failed to convince me that your salary is out of alignment with the market. I'm sorry, but there's nothing I can do about it right now.'*

Ron: *'That's disappointing. Okay, I'll need to consider what other options might be available to me.'*

Two days later…

Ron: *'Ivan, you know I said I would be considering other career options? Well, I've had an offer from Company A who are prepared to pay me 15% more than my current salary.'*

Ivan: *'Okay, I guess you've made your decision then. Company A are a good outfit, so I wish you all the best with them. I assume you will be working your full one-month notice. If you get a brief resignation letter to me by the end of today, then I'll pass it on to HR and we will get things moving. We can aim for a final work day of 31 days from now.'*

Ron: *'Wait… I didn't say I was resigning, just that I've received a better offer.'*

Ivan: *'Ron, you need to make your own decision. I hope you're not trying to use this as a way to get me to increase your salary — we've had that conversation and it's not going to happen. If you're trying to force my hand with a job offer, then it's not going to work. And, the fact that you've clearly been using time and energy to find a job with one of our competitors indicates a lack of loyalty, both to the organisation and to me as your manager. No, in fact, the more I think about it, the more I think it best that you leave sooner rather than later. You're now a liability to us from a competitive knowledge perspective.'*

SEQUEL

Ron handed his notice in the next morning.

The reason for the delay was that he had had a torrid day and a sleepless night, having had a blazing row with his wife in the meantime, and left his two small children crying as they did not know what was going on.

Ron did not have a job offer from Company A – it was a blatant lie. He had attended two interviews with Company A in the last few weeks, but the day before his initial conversation with Ivan he had been rejected from the recruitment process.

Ron was now in a big, deep, horrible hole – a hole he'd dug with his own spade. He had no job, just one-month's pay-off to live on; he had damaged his relationship with his boss and sullied his relationship with his company. The reason he handed in his resignation is because he's a bully who has been used to getting his own way. Also, as a bully, the thought of backing down was more than he could handle.

Three months later Ron was working as a shop assistant in an organic farm shop. He was earning about 30% of his previous salary.

INSIGHTS AND LEARNING

If you're going to call someone's bluff, then you had better be prepared to follow it through.

Using bluff is a legitimate negotiation tactic, though you need to be very brave, very confident, or at least be able to fake the confidence that comes from a powerful position, and you need to be prepared for it to backfire.

Ron did bluff. He did it with (fake) confidence and he calculated that the move would more likely work than not, as it would force his boss to make some improvement to his salary, even if not to fully match the 15%. After all, would his boss really be happy to lose him as a sales rep? Ron was good and he knew it.

We also wonder about Ivan's perspective.

Considering the speed with which Ivan was prepared to accept Ron's resignation, asking him to get the resignation letter to him by the end of the day, and the fact that Ivan did not even attempt to get into a negotiation with Ron, we wonder if the boss was secretly pleased. Maybe Ivan had been looking to get rid of Ron for some time. Brash bullies tend to cause other difficulties within an organisation that go beyond demanding high remuneration. Some of them may achieve great results, but at what cost and with what trail of destruction behind them?

Bluff does work when the other party believes what is said and feels they must act or concede in order to avoid a problem. It can also work if the other party thinks they're going to lose out on something, or they simply want to maintain the status quo.

Bluffing is, of course, a dangerous game, as the other person may call your bluff.

In the above case Ron left the organisation, in fact he left the very next day on one-month's pay due to the threat of keeping him in the company when he was (supposedly) going to a competitor. He had to leave the keys to his company car, return his laptop and he had no time to say goodbye to his former colleagues. The company paid for a taxi to take him home.

However, what if you bluff and you're found out, but you can't get out of the situation so quickly? In that case the damage can be fatal. Having bluffed and failed, you will be seen as a liar who is not to be trusted. You're also likely to fail in future attempted negotiations.

Once trust is broken, like a mirror, it's virtually impossible to reinstate.

HOW CAN I USE THIS?

If you do choose to use bluff, then, in addition to feigning confidence, you can say things like:

- *'I appreciate your offer, but it's too low, and I have someone else coming round to look at the car this afternoon – they seem very keen as they need a car by the end of the week.'*
- *'Thanks for your proposal, however, I know I can get this much cheaper elsewhere. If you can match their price, then I'll sign the paperwork now.'*
- *'If you do follow through with your threat, then I am going to counter it with X. It's up to you now – the ball's in your court. Don't put me in the position where I need to take the counteraction of X, as I will, and that won't be good for either of us.'*

Bluffing is lying. It's interesting from a psychological perspective that we all lie to some extent, yet we detest it and find it repugnant in others.

Rather than encouraging you to bluff or lie, perhaps a more positive contribution from this case is to help you to spot liars; you can do this from both what they say and the non-verbal signals that liars tend to display.

HOW TO SPOT LIARS NON-VERBALLY

- Contrary to popular belief, a liar does not always avoid eye contact; determined liars look you in the eye, leveraging the myth, to try to appear more sincere, i.e. *'I'm looking you in the eye, so I cannot be lying to you.'*
- Look for 'micro-signals' such as an increase in their rate of blinking, or 'micro-expressions' such as a fleeting smile, a momentary show of fear, contempt or disgust – expressions which are almost impossible to control.

- Watch for eye movements. If a right-handed person facing you looks up and to their right (your left), then there's more chance that they're lying or inventing something (the eye movements are reversed for a left-handed person) – it's not a cast-iron rule, but it's worth taking into account.

- Also contrary to popular belief, determined liars freeze their upper bodies to leverage the myth that liars fidget (hence, if they're still then they cannot be lying). Constrained gestures, folded arms, interlocked legs and lack of hand movements can be signs of not wanting to give information away.

- In trying too hard liars might fake gestures such as false smiles, when in fact a real smile, that cannot be faked, comes from the eyes not from the mouth.

- They may give incongruent headshakes (side to side) when affirming something, saying 'yes' or 'I'm more than happy to…' However, if you're culturally aware you will know that some nationalities, Indians for example, rock their head from side to side when they say, and mean, 'yes'.

- If they're not Indian, and they do nod their head, then a liar tends to hesitate with the nodding action when giving an answer; people telling the truth tend to nod before verbalising their response.

- Liars tend to put barrier objects between them and the other person.

- They may tend to lean away rather than towards the other person, or point their feet towards the door – an unconscious signal that they want to get away.

- People tend to sweat more when they lie, though, be careful, they may just be a sweaty person!

- Nose touching, mouth covering, and eye rubbing are also signs that something's not right and they may be lying; rubbing the back of their neck is a good indication that they're frustrated, and maybe trying to think their way out of a situation.

- Grooming behaviours such as fiddling with hair, a tie or cufflinks are also signals to be wary of. It can indicate nervousness; possibly because they're lying or at least feeling very uncomfortable.

- Liars may be constantly trying to lubricate their throat when lying by swallowing, gulping or clearing their throat.

HOW TO SPOT LIARS VERBALLY

- Firstly, liars tend to over-compensate and over-rehearse their verbal delivery when planning to lie, or when expecting to be questioned. They may come across as being over-determined to make their point, using more formal, moderated, paced and emphasised language, saying things like 'I did not do it' rather than the more usual and natural 'I didn't do it'.

- Over-prepared liars are also more likely to answer your questions immediately, as they've anticipated the question and have a rehearsed answer ready – which they're overly keen to deliver.

- Liars may try to speak in a lower vocal tone to try to sound more serious, sincere and commanding.

- If lying without preparation, they may be more hesitant, they may backtrack on what they say, stutter or stammer; the stress of the situation may make them start talking faster or slower than normal and their vocal pitch may rise or take on a quavering tone.

- Liars use a lot of 'qualifying language', such as *To be perfectly honest…*', *'I am not lying to you when I say…*', or *'I've always been brought up to tell the truth so…'*. Genuinely truthful people hardly ever feel the need to qualify their statements; they don't have to tell you they're telling the truth because to them it is obvious that they are.

- Liars may use stalling tactics such as asking for the question to be repeated, or commenting on how good the question is, or how glad they are to have been asked it (even though they're not), in order to buy them thinking time.

- Liars may try to deflect the question by saying things like, *'It depends what you mean by that'*, *'It's not as simple as a straight yes or no'* or *'Where did you get that information?'* They may also try to answer a question with a question of their own – again deflecting the focus from them and potentially buying time.

- Honest people are cooperative, open, willing to be open-minded and enthusiastic about brainstorming an issue or opportunity.

- Honest people tend to become angry when challenged. Liars, on the other hand, tend to become defensive, dismissive or show contempt for the challenger.

- When faced with someone you think is lying, become more curious, probe and ask lots of questions; in doing so, they're likely to trip themselves up.

- Ask about the same thing in different ways or ask them to explain it again.

- Additionally, just stare at them in disbelief, or use silence. Many liars will want to fill the silence, embellishing their story and possibly making a slip in the process. Don't interrupt; let them dig their own grave. If necessary, hand them a shovel!

34 GUILT TRIP

34 GUILT TRIP

Corporate customer:	(A buyer from a for-profit organisation) *'What? Are you seriously saying that's all you're offering? I cannot believe you're so devoid of moral fibre to insist on imposing that penalty. Do you realise the impact it will have on us? How will I explain this to the Board?'*
Charity customer:	(A buyer from a not-for-profit organisation) *'I'm looking for your support here, Katy. We're trying to raise money for those less fortunate, so I really need the best price you can offer... come on, it's for the kids!'*

INSIGHTS AND LEARNING

The guilt trip tactic (also referred to as 'Widows and Orphans') tries to appeal to the good nature, moral values and sympathies of the other party. It's difficult to argue with as nobody, other than psychopaths, want to hurt others (or at least be seen to be doing so) for personal gain.

In particular, nobody wants to be accused of directly or indirectly harming someone from a vulnerable or disadvantaged group, such as widows, orphans, homeless, unemployed or disabled.

HOW CAN I USE THIS?

Like some of the other tactics uncovered in this book, we are not necessarily advocating their use. However, you will find times when they're used on you or, in this case, where you might find yourself feeling sorry for the other party and, therefore, conceding much more or much more quickly than you would normally. That said, on occasion, if you believe the plea to be genuine, you do not apply a counter tactic at all, and you simply do what you can to help.

- If you do help out, make sure the other party knows this is a one-off exception on your part, one that you will almost certainly not be able to repeat in future – otherwise you may have set an unsustainable precedent.

- Make sure that you associate yourself personally with the gesture; people buy and sell from people, not from organisations, so the personal capital that you can derive from being associated with an act of generosity may pay off in future dealings with this person.

- Whilst remaining as empathetic as you can, keep a cool head and stay focused on the rational business case: *'I'm really sorry, Sarah, I'd love to be able to help you if I could, but in the current climate it's simply not possible.'*

- A harder line would be: *'Eric, we're not a charity, and neither is your organisation. I'm sorry, but I cannot mix up emotive issues with the business at hand. Can we please get back to discussing the terms of our deal?'*

- If all else fails, you can refer back to the contract, and if penalties do need to be imposed or a hard logical line followed, you have the letter of the law on your side. Just don't expect the contract to be renewed next year!

35 FUNNY MONEY

35 FUNNY MONEY

Sabrina:	'Mr Brandon, this policy, to protect you, your wife, and your two children, works out at just 50 Rand per day, so I'm sure you'll agree that's excellent value for money for the peace of mind it will provide.'
Andy:	'Sabrina, firstly, I know you're trying to be polite and professional, but please do call me Andy. Anyway, you say it's only 50 Rand per day, but by my calculations there are 365 days in most years and so that means 18,250 Rand per year, and considering we're a young family, my wife and myself are in very good health and nothing's likely to happen to us for the foreseeable future, that's a large amount of money you're asking me to commit to.'
Sabrina:	'Mr Brandon… err, sorry… Andy, I see your point, but when you do look at it on a cost per day basis, it's less than one pint of beer. Are you really saying that the welfare and security of your family is worth less than a pint of beer per day?'
Andy:	'Sabrina, firstly, I don't drink, and, secondly, demeaning this to such a crass comparison, after I just complimented you on being polite and professional, seems inappropriate. If I were to extend your analogy over an annual basis, then this policy equates to about 200 bottles of good quality South African Wine. Or, as I don't drink, it's equivalent to me having a meal in a nice restaurant with my wife every two weeks. I know which I would choose.'

INSIGHTS AND LEARNING

Sabrina wants to reduce the perceived cost of the life insurance policy and has chosen to do this by quoting it as a cost per day.

When quoting prices or asking for concessions, it's common for sellers to try to make what they're asking for seem small or trivial, for example, 'We're only talking about 2% more than you were expecting to pay', 'It's only $2 per unit price reduction on a $150 item' or 'It only amounts to €50 per day'.

Sellers will talk about monthly, weekly or daily costs, whereas what they're really proposing is an annual fee of many multiples of that. Alternatively, they may talk about low initial payments, when in fact the ramp up in future years becomes prohibitive.

Buyers will try to diminish the size of the discount they're requesting by saying it is only 2% when in fact the capital equipment costs $80 million, so they're really talking about a $1,600,000 discount. Gosh, that suddenly looks like a huge amount to give away!

What the other person is trying to do is to diminish the *absolute* amount (often cost) of what they're asking for, so as to make it, and perhaps you also, seem petty.

HOW CAN I USE THIS?

- As a seller, agreeing to a 5% price decrease on a major contract could actually wipe out 50% of your profit margin. If your profit is 10% then a 5% price reduction suddenly costs you 50% of your profit… ouch! Realise this and point it out to the other party.

- As a commercial buyer, not managing to secure a 5% discount on a high-value component could mean you need to increase your final end user sales price by more than the market will stand. Point this out to the other party.

- Clearly distinguish between absolute (e.g. cash amounts) and relative (percentage) values, and calculate what a certain % increase or decrease means in real terms. Apply this logic to all variables that involve a number.

- When buying, aggregate any small figures quoted into bigger timescales such as monthly, quarterly or annual costs – and play this back to the other party in these terms. Remember their 'small' €50 per day is more than a whopping €18,000 extra per year!

- When selling, break down big numbers into smaller, more palatable ones, as in, *'So, for just a few extra pounds a day you're getting the valuable added reassurance of the service contract.'*

- Remember, every concession you make costs you something – make this concession from you to the other party seem to be as big as possible, emphasise the value that you're handing over and how difficult it is for you to concede to it.

- Remember, every concession that you do not receive reduces the value of the deal to you – make this into a 'big deal', if not a deal-breaker, you should be able to push back to either obtain the concession, part of the concession, or something else to 'sweeten' the deal.

36 HIGHER AUTHORITY

36 HIGHER AUTHORITY

Emmanuelle: (Supplier to corporate customer N.) *'Valerie, I'm sorry, but that really is the very best price I can do for you on those predicted volumes.'*

Valerie: *'That's a shame, because I cannot possibly agree to the contract under those terms.'*

Emmanuelle: *'So, are you saying, that's it? We're going to get to the end of the current contract and you don't want to renew?'*

Valerie: *'You leave me no choice. I know I can get similar products for about 15% less than you're quoting, so unless you can do anything more on the price I'm compelled to go elsewhere.'*

Emmanuelle: *'Can you give me 24 hours? I am at the limit of what I am allowed to agree, but it may be that if I speak to my regional director he'll sanction a further price concession. I can't promise anything, but will you at least give me 24 hours to see what I can do?'*

Valerie: *'That's fine, Emmanuelle – can you get back to me by the end of tomorrow?'*

24 hours later, Emmanuelle came back to Valerie to say that it had been tough, but she had managed to secure a further 10% price reduction. There absolutely could be nothing more and that she hoped that Valerie would be happy to proceed on that basis, knowing that they have a long-standing relationship and that it would inevitably involve some disruption and supply risk if Valerie were to go to another, unknown supplier.

Valerie accepted the new offer and thanked Emmanuelle for taking the time and making the effort to improve the deal by negotiating internally herself.

Valerie did not want to go to a new supplier, but would have done if Emmanuelle had not made any concession on the price. 10% was sufficient for Valerie, as she also knew that the extra 5% cost saving would be eaten up with the cost of switching suppliers.

INSIGHTS AND LEARNING

Playing the 'higher authority' tactic means you state you're unable to agree to a concession or make a final decision because you need approval from someone more senior in your organisation.

Of course it does not need to be in a corporate context. If you are negotiating personally with a tour operator, exploring holiday options, you may say something like… *'Well, it seems to be a reasonable deal to me, but the real person you and I need to convince is my wife! It's going to be difficult to persuade her unless you can include the free daily breakfasts and city tour that you mentioned were additional expenses.'*

Advantages of using this tactic are:

- You can excuse yourself from making a concession or agreeing to something right now.
- It buys you time to think and to consider what else you can do to configure the deal to make it more palatable to the other party.
- Very importantly, it allows you to save face if and when you do come back with a better offer; you're using the greater powers of the 'higher authority', usually a more senior decision maker, to be able to say, *'You knew I could not go any further, but I've received the go-ahead from my boss.'*
- You can use it in cases when you do have the ability to agree to the other party's request or demand, but you want to put pressure on them by making them think that what they're asking for is beyond what is reasonable. Alternatively, you may just want to make them sweat it out for a few days, hoping that they're likely to be even more desperate to agree a deal when you do come back to them, either with a slightly better offer or even the same deal.

Disadvantages of using this tactic are:

- It can make you look impotent and unimportant.
- You undermine your own position for future negotiations, and you may be bypassed in future as the other party may just go direct to your boss.
- If you're playing the higher authority card deliberately, and not entirely truthfully, be prepared to take the consequences of your deception. For example, the other party may call your bluff and go ahead and deal with someone else in the period of your manufactured delay.

Of course, this may not be a tactic at all. One party may indeed have no choice but to admit that they genuinely need to check in with other people before making a commitment.

HOW CAN I USE THIS?

- Prevention is far better than having to deal with difficult situations when they happen; so always establish the authority level of the person(s) you're negotiating with before you get into serious discussions or invest too much time.
- Ask, *'If we can reach an agreement today, do you have the authority to agree the*

deal on behalf of your organisation?' If *'yes'*, then proceed; if *'no'* or *'in principle'*, then respectfully ask that the final decision-maker or group be involved from the start, or ask for clarification about what 'in principle' means.

If you have not prevented the situation arising and you now face a higher authority situation, then:

- Politely indicate that in the interests of time, for all concerned, you would like to negotiate directly with those who are in a position to make a decision, whilst reassuring the other party that you're in a position to make an agreement.

- Say you're disappointed to only now find yourself in this position, and that you will withdraw from further discussion until the right people are in the room.

- Accept their stance, but say that as this is now escalating you will also now need to bring in more senior people from your organisation to conclude the deal.

- State the exact conditions upon which you're prepared to sign the contract and say that if the 'higher authority' is prepared to go ahead on that basis, then they have a deal – effectively you're laying down a 'gauntlet' (see Part Two), asking the other party to engage in their own internal negotiations and to come back to you with their acceptance, otherwise you will walk away.

37 GOOD COP, BAD COP

37 GOOD COP, BAD COP

Mother:	'Jamie, have you finished your assignment?'
Jamie:	'Mum, I wish you'd stop pestering me. I'll get round to it some time.'
Mother:	'But Jamie, it's due in on Monday morning and the last time you showed it to me you'd only done about a third of it. You're not going get it finished in time at this rate.'
Jamie:	'Like I said, I wish you'd stop going on about it. Even if I miss the deadline, I know people who have managed to negotiate an extension.'
Mother:	'Is that the mentality you're approaching this with... you'll deliberately miss the deadline as you know you might get an extension? So, what if they don't give you an extension, and what if even then you find you can't finish it in time because you run out of time again, get a brain freeze or are ill or something?'
Jamie:	'Mum, will you get out of my room – I don't want to talk about it any more.'
Mother:	'Jamie, you're 15 years old and responsible for your own school work. I can't force you to do your assignment, but I wouldn't want to be in your shoes when dad gets home at 7pm. I can tell you now the first thing he's going to ask you about is the progress you've made with your assignment. You know how he reacted on Tuesday, and it's now Friday, he's going to go ballistic if you can't show him you're serious about this and have made significant progress. Look, it's only 2pm now. You have five hours to apply yourself. Come on, Jamie, I don't want to be around to see dad's reaction if you can't show him something that is at least two-thirds complete.'

Note, you may have detected a similarity between what is happening above, and the previous case about 'higher authority'.

INSIGHTS AND LEARNING

Famously demonstrated in US cop shows, 'good cop, bad cop', or 'good guy, bad guy' is one of the oldest, best-known and most quoted negotiation tactics.

In a meeting with two or more people from the other side, one person behaves in a difficult manner, asking challenging and confrontational questions, making high demands and appearing less interested in negotiating a mutually agreeable solution. They may even become aggressive and make threats. Their role is to create an uncomfortable tension and to put pressure on you.

But then another person steps in and takes a much more pleasant and agreeable approach. The 'good cop' may even apologise for the 'bad cop's' behaviour, but they appeal to the other party to be reasonable and to comply because if they do not, then the bad cop may make things very unpleasant. Whereas the bad cop causes tension, the good cop creates a source of escape and resolution, or the promise of avoidance of pain.

An interesting twist is when the same person plays both good and bad cop – the negotiation equivalent of Jekyll and Hyde! One minute they're demanding and aggressive, and then they calm down and appeal to reason. You may at that point be tempted to concede to prevent the bad cop re-emerging.

In the example above the father was not even present, but the mother was using the threat of the dad's likely reaction to negotiate with her son. By the time the father returned, sure enough, the first thing he asked Jamie about was his assignment. Jamie had been working on it for the last five hours and was able to show his dad, though with a degree of nervousness, a well-advanced piece of work.

We privately know that at 6pm the mother telephoned her husband to tell him what had been happening, that Jamie had made significant progress, and for the dad not to be too hard on him when he came home.

This also illustrates the point that the good cop and the bad cop are both on the same 'side' – something that is explored below.

HOW CAN I USE THIS?

- Professional negotiators generally do not advocate you use this technique or, if you do, use it sparingly and be aware that it's a well-known tactic. Therefore, be prepared to have your cover blown or maybe even ridiculed in the process.

- Whenever a nasty tactic is exposed it loses most, if not all, of its power. So, if you find this approach used on you, expose them for what they're doing; they know they're trying to pressurise you into conceding something, so the best thing is to let them know that it's not going to work on you.

- Remind yourself that they're both on the same side, and they both have an interest in getting you to do what the bad cop wants. So, even if you do not expose their behaviour, decide internally that you will not let it influence you.

- Negotiate with the 'good cop' as though they were the 'bad cop', because they're both bad guys really. Don't let the supposedly nice behaviour of one of them unduly influence you, be tough and resilient with both of them.

- Use their behaviour to undermine them, but without exposing their technique.

Say, 'Look guys, it seems the two of you are not fully aligned in terms of approach or what you want. Why don't we take a break to give you chance to discuss amongst yourselves and then we can resume the negotiation?'

- Use humour (but be very careful with this one): 'Oh no... not the old "good cop, bad cop routine!" I thought we'd moved on from 1970's police dramas. Next thing, you'll be dressing up in uniform!'

38 LAYING DOWN A MARKER

38 LAYING DOWN A MARKER

Carl: (Salesman from supplier P.) *'Francois, good to meet you, and thanks for your enquiry. I understand that you're interested in putting in place a vendor-managed inventory and logistics management process.'*

Francois: (Lead Buyer from customer Q.) *'Yes, but before we get too far into discussions I need to have a rough idea of how much all of this is likely to cost, both on an initial set-up and an on-going annual basis.'*

Carl: *'Wow, I totally understand the question, but it's one that's impossible to answer until I know more about your operation and what you're trying to achieve.'*

Francois: *Well, I know that you do this for company R on the same business park. We're roughly the same size as their operation and I cannot imagine that our requirements would be much different. Just assume we're like company R – what ball park figures are we likely to be looking at?'*

Carl: *'Francois, I wish it were that simple. Can I ask how much budget you have for this – both for initial start-up and then annual on-going costs?'*

Francois: *'We don't have a ring-fenced or defined budget. We just know that this is the direction we want to go in. Clearly, we're looking for value for money, but we're not the experts in this area – you are. Surely you're able to give me some idea of likely costs? You do this all the time – it's your job!'*

Carl: *'If I did try to estimate, then it'd be with a very rough finger stuck in the air and with a strong gale blowing from all directions – I am not sure how helpful that would be.'*

Francois: (Laughing.) *'I don't care how rough your finger is, or the state of the weather right now, just give me a rough estimate – are we talking about tens of thousands or closer to a million?'*

This 'dance' carried on for some time. Both parties were refusing to do what, in negotiation parlance, is called 'laying down a marker' (see Part Two).

INSIGHTS AND LEARNING

A 'marker' is a stated position, usually numerical, such as price or volume.

When you lay down a 'marker' you put a line in the sand, a starting point, a request, a demand or an offer. For example, a seller may say *'We charge £1,200 per day for project management,* a buyer may say *'We're looking at a maximum target* price of €32.00 per unit', a seller may say 'We don't supply any quantities below 1,000 units', a buyer may say 'I need you to understand that our payment terms are 90 days month end from receipt of invoice.'

These are all examples of markers; they almost sound non-negotiable, but good negotiators know that everything is negotiable.

In the above example, Carl was probably right in refusing to give a price, even an estimate, without knowing much more about the situation and what the prospective client wanted to achieve. No two clients for bespoke services are ever alike – that's the nature of bespoke.

Equally, maybe Francois really did not have a defined budget, yet he would have been reluctant to reveal this even if he did. Imagine if Francois had said, 'Well, we probably have around €1 million to invest in year one, and then a further €700,000 for each of the following years.' A smart Carl, who may be thinking it would cost about two-thirds of that amount, would say something like, 'Okay, I think that's within reach. If we can implement that for you within your budget, would you be prepared to go ahead in principle?'

HOW CAN I USE THIS?

- A good rule of thumb is to try not to be the first person to lay down a marker; try to get the other party to state their position first. This gives you information about the 'L' of their LIM strategy (what, in an ideal world, they would Like to achieve) and you can then choose how to respond. (See Part Two and case 39 – 'LIM Strategy' for more information.)

- Sellers generally want to find out how much buyers are prepared to pay and they often ask about available budget. If you're a buyer, you don't need to tell them. They're the vendors and they know their prices, so simply ask them to submit a fair proposal.

- However, there are times when you may want to state your position first, particularly if you want to precondition the other party, because where you start sets expectations in their minds.

- Before you even get to the marker stage do your research; what does the market or independent benchmarks say about what's reasonable? Establish the zone of acceptability and then start at the edge, or even outside of this, and move in, as appropriate as the other party also makes concessions.

- If you do need, or want, to lay down a marker, then aim high (seller) or low (buyer). Make sure your position is stretching and realistic because unrealistic demands make you look either out of touch or stupid.

- If and when you do move from your original position, move reluctantly, slowly and modestly. A large, early move shows you were originally way out of the ballpark and, more damagingly, that you probably still have far more to give.

- Avoid making a series of moves one after the other. If you've already moved several times on one or more variables, it implies you can, and will, move again.

- Try to get the other party to be the first to move their marker in your direction. If they do make their move without making it conditional on some other concession from you, then they've moved and you haven't; the gap has now narrowed in your favour.

- Golden rule… always insist on a concession from the other party, on another variable that's important to you, as a condition of you moving your marker from its original position.

39 LIM STRATEGY

39 LIM STRATEGY

Graham: 'Yeah, I entered the London Marathon this year and they've accepted my application. Now it's really happening I'm nervous about it. I've never run a full marathon before. I don't even know if I am capable of running more than 26 miles.'

Trevor: 'That's great, Graham, well done. I had my application rejected this year. I don't know if it's because I've already run it two years in three, so they give new applicants a chance, but I'm really pleased for you – it's a day you'll remember for the rest of your life. What targets have you set yourself?'

Graham: 'What do you mean by 'targets'? I thought there was only one target, i.e. how long it takes from start to finish line, or maybe you're thinking my target should be to at least get around before the follow-up vehicle comes round to pick up the traffic cones!'

Trevor: 'Ha! No. I was thinking you should set yourself targets at three levels. The most stretching target should be the fastest time that you'd like to complete the 26.2 miles; the slowest time you would be prepared to accept would be your lowest, least stretching target, but it's still a target; and then you'd have another target, somewhere in-between, which is the time you think is your most likely time to finish.'

INSIGHTS AND LEARNING

Trevor has just helped Graham to set himself a LIM strategy.

LIM stands for Like, Intend and Must.

1. What he would **L**ike to achieve   - his ideal goal, his fastest time to complete.
2. What he **I**ntends to achieve   - his most realistic, or expected time.
3. What he **M**ust achieve   - his absolute maximum time to complete the race.

However, it's not only about time. In any negotiation, as in a marathon, there are several variables that make up the 'negotiation mix'.

In a commercial negotiation, in addition to price you might negotiate around quantity, quality, delivery, phasing, payment terms, packaging, after-care or additional services… to name just a few.

HOW CAN I USE THIS?

For your next negotiation:

- Brainstorm all the significant variables that are important in this negotiation.
- Set yourself LIM targets for *each variable*.
- Step back and consider how these variables and targets are interdependent.
- Consider which of these you're prepared to move on, i.e. to be flexible in terms of bargaining, and which are non-negotiable.
- Consider which variables, if any, you're prepared to forego if you get what you want in other, more important variables – remember, it's about the 'whole deal'.
- Consider everything and map out a range of acceptable outcome scenarios.
- Stick to your LIM – unless external factors shift substantially, in which case re-evaluate and set yourself a new LIM strategy.

40 CREATIVITY CREATES A BREAKTHROUGH

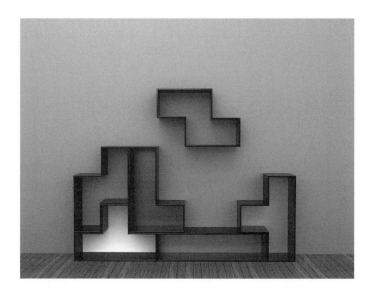

40 CREATIVITY CREATES A BREAKTHROUGH

Philip is a Key Account Manager for manufacturing business Q. He manages relationships with a number of purchasers from Do It Yourself (DIY) and other retailers, including one of the largest DIY retailers in the UK, Company R.

Business Q is the lead supplier in one of Company R's categories; they've been trusted partners for more than 20 years.

Philip knows that his organisation also has competency in another supply category, and he's been trying to secure this additional line of business with the retailer for many years, so far unsuccessfully.

Philip is perplexed as to why this is and has become frustrated in the process – he thinks he's tried everything.

Over the last five years Philip has:

- Negotiated significant price reductions to try to tempt Company R to take their other product line.
- Offered different design variants to help them improve their product range and the appeal of Company R's offerings to its end customers.
- Suggested a range of different trading terms.
- Offered flexible delivery and/or stock level options in order to optimise the supply chain and minimise costs to Company R.
- Offered cash incentives and rebates.
- Offered extended payment terms.
- Offered favourable settlement discounts.

Everything he has tried has so far failed.

Philip is close to giving up.

The reason he's been given is that the incumbent supplier is doing an excellent job and, even though Philip's proposals have been attractive, changing the supplier is viewed by the purchaser as an 'unnecessary risk'.

Philip knew that, although the category he was targeting was important for the retailer, it did have a major drawback. The products were bulky and of irregular shape, making them difficult to display efficiently. This meant that sales densities were very low for the retailer, reducing their profit per square metre.

Philip thought creatively about this and wondered if his company could develop and supply a bracket to be fixed on to Company R's existing in-store shelving that would increase the number of products that would fit within a one-metre bay, and at the same time, displaying them more effectively to the browsing public.

This relatively simple, but revolutionary change in thinking and approach moved the negotiation away from the conventional (and hereto unproductive) battleground of product and price, into a new arena, where Philip was able to solve a problem that had been taken for granted by Company R as unsolvable.

This solution enabled the retailer to increase their sales densities in the same space by a whopping 53% – overnight!

Not only did Philip finally win the business from his competitor, he also secured the exclusive rights from Company R to the entire category, and he negotiated a guaranteed three-year deal. The purchaser was also delighted with the breakthrough in thinking and significant increase in sales. She even took Philip out for a couple of drinks at the end of their day, as he had helped her make a significant inroad in achieving her own corporate objectives, one of which is monetary sales per square metre.

INSIGHTS AND LEARNING

In thinking differently about the situation, and by standing back and asking himself the question 'What could make the purchaser change her mind?,' Philip was able to achieve a breakthrough in thinking, which led to dramatically positive results – for both parties.

He successfully differentiated his category proposal from the competition and, most importantly, from the current incumbent supplier.

We learn from this case that persistence can pay off – in this instance, in a hugely beneficial way.

However, we also learn that persistence is not helpful if you're simply banging your head, in the same way, against the same brick wall. Philip had been persistent for years, but he was not thinking creatively enough, or rather he was not thinking outside of the traditional variables of price, volume, discounts, etc.

So, there's a message here about the importance of applying truly creative, intelligent effort, rather than just continuing to push in the same way. Creative thinking in a negotiation can be just the spark that's needed to get the negotiation moving again, in a different and far more productive direction.

There's also a message here about questioning and listening in order to understand the deeper situation and the underlying, fundamental, and often not always spoken, needs of the other party.

Questioning and listening should be two of the sharpest tools in the negotiator's toolbox – they're not to be underestimated.

HOW CAN I USE THIS?

- If what you're doing isn't working, then try something else, almost anything else, so long as it's something else.

- If you're continually encountering a block or resistance, then you need to step out of the situation and ask yourself why this is happening, particularly if it's occurring repeatedly, either with the same party or with many others.

- Test your own assumptions; maybe you need to recalibrate.

- Maybe your expectations are unrealistic. Maybe, if you're totally honest with yourself, and you've exhausted all possibilities you can think of, this deal or situation really is not going to fly; your time and efforts might be better expended elsewhere.

- Keep your mind, eyes and ears open at all stages of a negotiation. Don't skim over this point, it is critical. Having your 'radar' on at all times is crucial.

- Don't be afraid to probe for different needs. If you don't ask, then you're unlikely to discover what's really important to the other party from either a needs/wants perspective or a benefits/problem-elimination view. In the above case study, the buyer had a problem that she had simply accepted could not be solved, and so she had never even bothered to raise it with Philip.

- As mentioned, the most important skills in the early stage of a negotiation are questioning and listening. Resist the temptation to make too many statements or demands; ask, be quiet, listen and make notes.

- The person asking the questions is usually the person who's in control, and by 'asking' more than 'telling', you gain valuable information during the early stages of the negotiation. We all know that 'information is power'… it's just a shame it took Philip five years to get to that point.

- When you're stuck in a negotiation, at a perceived impasse, appeal to the other party to work with you to jointly create multiple options and to explore additional possibilities, alternatives, options and choices.

- As has been mentioned previously, in the Introduction and in cases 17 and 22, if you believe you only have one 'pie' and you take more than 50%, it means the other person gets less. The approach of creating multiple options is not about dividing a single pie, what's often termed a 'zero-sum game', but more about making the pie bigger, as Philip did in this case when he thought creatively about reconfiguring the 'pie'.

- The goal is for you to maximise the 'pie' using cooperation, information sharing and mutual problem-solving. This approach creates value, since both parties leave the negotiation feeling they have achieved greater value for themselves than before.

41 BLOODY MINDEDNESS

41 BLOODY MINDEDNESS

Eric: (Ray's Lawyer.) *'Ray, my job's to defend you against the prosecutors. You're telling me, and I have no reason to disbelieve you, that it was not you who broke your daughter's arm. However, the defence lawyer for your wife is saying that it wasn't her. So, if your wife's telling the truth, then it must have been you, because what you both do agree on is that the only three people in the house at the time were you, your wife and your daughter. Either you're telling the truth or she is – it had to be one of you.'*

Ray: *'Eric, I swear to God it wasn't me. I was downstairs and my wife was upstairs when I heard Kayleigh scream. I'm telling you, she's lying.'*

Eric: *'How would you describe your relationship with your wife? I mean before this incident happened? Were you getting on, or were there problems?'*

Ray: *'It's been strained; we argue. It's not fair on the kid. The only thing I can think is she's using this as a way to get back at me, and as Kayleigh suffered temporary concussion due to the fall, and can't remember what happened or who was with her, I'm stuffed.'*

24 hours later…

Eric: *'Ray, there are four ways forward. Either you admit to child harm, or your wife does. I can't imagine you conspired with your wife to break Kayleigh's arm together.'*

Ray: *'But I didn't do it – it must have been her! …You said there were four options.'*

Eric: *'Yes, the third is you declare your innocence, and if your wife does the same, it will be left for the judge to decide who is to blame. In your favour is the fact that you claim that you were downstairs when you heard Kayleigh scream and, due to your own broken leg, you could not get upstairs. Supporting your wife's case is the fact that it was she who drove Kayleigh to hospital – though, admittedly, you could not have done so because your leg was in a plaster cast. With this third option, because neither of you are pleading guilty, the sentence is likely to be more severe for the party judged to be culpable. If you're innocent and are found guilty, then that would be what we call 'rough justice'. If you're guilty and your wife is found guilty instead,… well, I would question your ability to be able to sleep at night for many months afterwards.*

The fourth option, which I have discussed with the prosecution, is called "plea bargaining". Basically, it means that both you and your wife admit to a lesser

*charge of "child neglect" – you share the non-attributable blame. That's likely
to result in some form of mutual penalty. It would not result in a custodial
sentence for either you or your wife – it would probably be a fine and it would
certainly mean that you both receive a criminal record.*

*If you can't sort this out with your wife, my recommendation would be that you
jointly take the fourth option. Yes, there would be a penalty to both of you, but
it would be far less if it were to go to trial and one of you were subsequently
to be convicted.*

*If you're really innocent, then you would be a fool to admit guilt. If you're lying
to me, then you should admit the offence and hope that the judge will give you
a lesser penalty for coming clean, which is what normally happens but which
I cannot guarantee.'*

24 hours later…

Ray and his wife both agreed to submit a plea of joint culpability against the charge
of 'child neglect'. The judge imposed a penalty that involved a £2,000 fine and a
community order on both Ray and his wife which involved attending parenting
re-alignment classes.

Of course, it has never since transpired which of the parents broke the child's arm.

INSIGHTS AND LEARNING

There are no winners in a case like this.

Kayleigh suffered a broken arm.

Each of her parents received a penalty of a fine and joint community order.

Their relationship suffered massively as a result and, five months later, Ray and his
wife separated; Kayleigh now lives with her mother.

Details aside, a case like this shows us that if two opposing parties are determined
to dig their heels in and fight to the bitter end, then it is not uncommon for both
to suffer. It is also possible that other 'innocent' bystanders are harmed in the
process.

In commercial negotiations it is not unknown for two parties to stubbornly dig
their heels in, make demands, refuse to budge and try to pressure the other party
to accede. Such situations rarely end well.

Pride, ego and bloody mindedness get in the way. The 'red mist' comes down and
people can then find themselves pursuing a path that they know will be destructive

to both parties. Even though they know they themselves are likely to come out damaged, they'll take some pleasure from seeing the other person suffer too.

When relationships break down, communication dries up or becomes adversarial and trust is lost, then there's a good chance that all hope is lost too, unless mediation can save the day.

In this case, Eric probably enabled Ray and his wife to achieve the least worst outcome, and, in some negotiations, damage limitation may be the best that can be achieved.

Kayleigh's arm was broken, but it could have been worse. Both parents suffered a penalty, but it could have been worse.

Perhaps this is the best that anyone could have hoped for from an already bad situation.

HOW CAN I USE THIS?

Firstly, don't get into the situation in the first place; easier said than done.

Secondly, learn to recognise when you might be slipping into a situation that is likely to end in a lose-lose outcome, and do what you can at that point to arrest the slide.

Other things that you can do include:

- Avoid the conflict as it arises by simply walking away if the matter is really not worth the argument or the time, stress and expense that it is likely to entail.
- Bring in others to handle the situation – perhaps a higher authority or someone with different knowledge, expertise or even a different perspective on the matter.
- Appeal to fairness, reasonable conduct and basic human values.
- Make a concession yourself in order to try to de-intensify the atmosphere and show willing in the hope that your concession will be reciprocated in some way.
- Try to get back into a bargaining or true negotiation-style atmosphere rather than a personal or emotionally charged one.
- Point out that you both seem to be heading for a lose-lose outcome and that maybe the best thing right now is to stop the escalation and emotion, agree on a compromise or a 'split the difference' type of approach, so you both at least come out with something that is not ideal, but is better than where you're both heading.

- Step back and try to clarify common needs and goals – there must be something that you can both agree upon, such as in this case, 'we agree not to do anything else that might harm Kayleigh any more'.
- Take, and encourage from the other party, very small steps in order to begin to rebuild trust – very hard, of course, if trust has broken down, but it *is* possible, and others have successfully come through traumatic events such as are portrayed in this case.

42 NEGOTIATING FROM ROCK BOTTOM

42 NEGOTIATING FROM ROCK BOTTOM

Carlos is concerned.

He's the business development manager for Manufacturing Mammoth, a company that supplies products to major retailers throughout Europe.

Carlos thought he was the lead supplier to REX, for the particular type of products they manufacture, and they have been trusted trading partners for at least 10 years.

Recently, however, Carlos has seen a marked decline in the level of business from REX, which coincided with Peter taking over as the lead buyer of his products.

It quickly became evident that Peter placed little value on the legacy relationship that REX had with Manufacturing Mammoth, and he did not appear to appreciate the added value that Carlos' business had offered in the past, and was continuing to offer.

Even worse, despite gradually moving parts of Carlos' existing business to competitor suppliers, the new buyer still negotiated hard for improved trading terms and insisted on better pricing on the now diminishing business volume with Manufacturing Mammoth.

In an attempt to avoid being viewed as confrontational, and wishing to help Peter with his own internal objectives and reputation, Carlos acceded to some of the demands. He did this in the hope that Peter's initially strong stance would soften and the mutual relationship would improve in the longer term.

However, as time passed, Peter's demands intensified whilst the business value to Manufacturing Mammoth continued to shrink. Even more worryingly, the relationship between Peter and Carlos became increasing strained and disengaged.

The REX account represented a significant chunk of Carlos' total business turnover; sales that Manufacturing Mammoth could ill-afford to lose. However, Carlos recognised that the relationship had reached a critical point and he had to make a strategic decision. Should he say nothing and suffer in silence because the risk of speaking out is too great, or should he take a firm stand on principle?

Carlos had a few stiff drinks one night; he discussed the situation with his wife, who, at one point said to him, *'Carlos, are you a man or a mouse? For goodness sake, you can't let this b*****d walk all over you!'*

This was the turning point for his decision. He decided to be firm. If nothing else, he had to show his wife that he was strong.

However, the next morning he took care to present his position, and that of his manufacturing organisation, as positively as possible.

He acknowledged absolutely that it was Peter's right to choose where to place his business, but also that it was their choice as supplier to allocate resources and support as appropriate for their own business. Fair is fair, action and reaction, demand and response, challenge and defence, sanction and counter sanction…

Carlos laid out all the marketing support, advertising, funding and account staff that he would now be disproportionately reducing to reflect the reduced size of business with REX. He made it very clear that he and his company were fully prepared to accept the consequences of this, but that he could no longer tolerate demands for additional concessions whilst the business with REX continued to shrink.

Peter's response, whilst not immediate, was both surprising and rewarding.

Within a month of declaring his position, Carlos was invited to pitch exclusively for a sizeable new business opportunity in which he was able to negotiate more favourable trading terms and secure price increases for two of his company's core ranges.

Carlos' relationship with Peter improved markedly, as did his access to the buying team.

Carlos' wife was very happy for him, and he felt proud for standing up for himself in the face of a corporate bully.

INSIGHTS AND LEARNING

Firstly, some people will try to bully the other party, yes, even in so-called 'professional' negotiation settings.

Secondly, Carlos made the mistake of giving in too soon and, by so doing, showed that he could be pushed around (though of course he later redeemed the situation).

Thirdly, he made the classic mistake of making concessions without asking for anything in return.

Fourthly, Carlos did push back, and when he did he was cool, unemotional, logical and he pointed out the natural consequences of Peter continuing along this path. This was a very wise, assertive and commendable path to take.

Finally, Carlos demonstrated that if Peter did not like it, then he would be prepared to walk away from the deal and the relationship would end. Well done, Carlos!

So, how can we learn from both Carlos' mistakes and his positive actions?

HOW CAN I USE THIS?

Firstly, do not allow yourself to be bullied.

Easier said than done. However, in any adult-to-adult negotiation don't give in to demands without asking for something in return. Meet demands with counter demands. Say you may be able to do B, but only on the express condition that the other party can do C. Make all of their demands conditional on them reciprocating in some way that has value to you.

Maybe Carlos' first mistake was to accede without asking for something in return, such as a higher unit volume, better payment terms or a longer contract, etc.

After Carlos gave in to a couple of requests, Peter's demands intensified. Could it be that in seeing Carlos appease, Peter regarded him as weak, and thought that if he got X last time he can demand twice X this time? Thus, Carlos was inadvertently 'training' Peter that if he bullied him, then Peter would get what he wanted. It's little wonder that Peter pushed for more the next time around.

If the other party does not value and respect your relationship, then do you really want to be doing business with this person? Probably not. Life's too short, and there are plenty of nicer kids to play with in the playground!

Whilst Carlos clearly wanted to protect the relationship, and he even acceded to some demands in the hope that the new relationship would improve, there comes a point when he has to protect his own interests, and those of his company. This is especially the case if the other party is being unreasonable, overly demanding, aggressive, hostile or even acting in a bullying manner.

Be prepared to walk away. This negotiation could have ended differently, but Carlos was prepared for any outcome and, as we know who Carlos is in real life, we know that he had the backing of his boss. So, whilst from the outside it might have looked like a bold move, Carlos felt confident and secure in pushing back. Carlos knew he could walk away and still keep his job.

Strength in position, knowing you have the support and backing of those above you, gives you considerable confidence to hold your ground in tough negotiation situations.

Finally, as illustrated by Carlos' story, a few glasses of wine in the evening, time to reflect with wives, husbands, partners, whomever, can be very helpful in clarifying matters and crystallising decisions in negotiations!

You have to draw upon all of the tools in your negotiation toolkit – in moderation.

43 LOYALTY OVER TRUTH

43 LOYALTY OVER TRUTH

Sean woke up in the police station, hung over and worse for wear.

Last night he had been in a nightclub and found himself in an argument with another customer. A scuffle had taken place, the end result being that the other customer was punched in the face and suffered a bloodied, but not broken, nose.

Sean knew he did not punch the guy – it was his brother, who had come to Sean's defence. However, in the scuffle and darkness of the nightclub, and with most people intoxicated with alcohol, nobody could say for certain who threw the punch.

Sean had his solicitor present – he wanted to know what was likely to happen now, and what the consequences might be.

His solicitor said that if he denied the charge, then the police would decide whether or not to pursue it further; it would be either a 'slap on the wrist' or it could go to court and potentially may involve a far more serious sentence. As this was actual bodily harm rather than grievous bodily harm then the sentence would be unlikely to be custodial, but it would certainly involve a penalty such as a large fine and/or community service and a criminal record.

If Sean admitted it, then the police were more likely to let him off with a severe caution, though he would still have a criminal record. However, as Sean was claiming that it was his brother who inflicted the harm, his solicitor strongly advised him to tell the truth and let his brother account for himself.

Against his solicitor's advice, Sean decided to admit culpability.

He received a £2,000 fine and a criminal record.

Three months later when he lost his job (not related to the case), his brother gave him a non-returnable 'loan' of £10,000 until he managed to find new employment.

INSIGHTS AND LEARNING

Why would an innocent person admit to a crime that they know someone else committed and take a criminal record on their behalf?

Because Sean did not want to get his brother into trouble, because his brother had come to his rescue, and because he knew that if his brother got a criminal record it would potentially be the end of his career as a teacher.

This case could be said to be unjust and unfair. After all, an innocent person has taken the blame, and the guilty party has got off free. An innocent person now has a criminal record and a violent teacher continues to teach.

However, ask yourself: was Sean entirely innocent? He did engage in a fight with another person, by his own admission that he consumed a lot of alcohol, and he was involved in the instigation of the situation that resulted in a punch in the face.

This shows that, on occasion, an individual can make decisions that harm them in order to help another party.

In business this would be rare, but when family, friends and other valued relationships are involved loyalty can trump logic; allegiance can overrule lucid judgement.

Several years ago in the UK, Chis Huhne, then Secretary of State for Energy and Climate Change, persuaded (negotiated with) his wife, Vicky Price, to admit that she was driving their family car after a speed camera had caught them. After going to court Mr Huhne changed his plea to guilty. Both he and his wife were jailed for perverting the course of justice.

HOW CAN I USE THIS?

We're certainly not advocating lying. However, there are times in less extreme negotiation situations when taking a short-term 'hit' can result in a longer-term benefit.

For example, in a negotiation team it may be that one of your colleagues has made a mistake or not delivered something on time, but as the more senior member of the team you decide to take responsibility for it in order to 'protect' your colleague, and strengthen your internal relationship with them.

It may be that in a negotiation you admit a mistake to the party on the other side, even if you know that it is debatable as to whether it was your fault or theirs. For example, you may say, *'Look, clearly there's been a misunderstanding here, and I'm prepared to admit that I could perhaps have worded it better – I can see how you might have misinterpreted it.'*

You do this either because you do not believe it's worth arguing about, you want to move things on, you want to preserve or build the relationship or because you're trying to build personal capital which you can then use as leverage in negotiating the much more important final outcome.

This case also illustrates the power of reciprocity (see the Reciprocity case in this book), as when Sean was in trouble his brother immediately stepped in to help.

He was probably desperate to repay his debt to Sean in some way. People are like elephants… they have long memories!

Loyalty also shows itself in other commercial negotiations, for example when a supplier provides a product or service to a 'friend' at what are sometimes called 'mates rates'. It's not necessarily bad or corrupt; it's just the way of the world. There's often an expectation that if you give a friend some business, or you're supplying someone in your close personal network, that more 'favourable' terms will be involved between the two parties.

At a more corporate level we also see this phenomenon in 'reciprocal trade deals'. These are perfectly above board and quite common in business.

44 VALUE DISCOVERY

44 VALUE DISCOVERY

Linhua, an industrial purchaser based in China, buys wooden pallets from a number of suppliers, some of them local, others international, both big and small.

Linhua needs to transport heavy goods around the world and so, whilst pallets might appear to the casual observer to be simple constructions of roughly hewn wood and nails, they're important components of his supply chain. The pallet supply business is highly competitive.

Ask yourself now… how many important variables can you think of in both the product (wooden pallets) and the broader negotiation about their supply?

Price is the first thing you may think of, but try to come up with another 14 variables.

Linhua discovered 24 sources of cost and/or value in this situation and so, rather than just reading what he came up with, you will benefit far more from this case if you try to discover 15 or more of these sources of value or 'variables' for yourself.

If you've written down 15, you now deserve to review Linhua's list of 24:

1. The unit cost per pallet.
2. The unit cost per pallet if he were to commit to higher volumes.
3. The pallet design.
4. Pallet strength and durability.
5. Pallet aesthetics.
6. Expected number of uses of the pallet before being destroyed/recycled.
7. Sourced from sustainable forests or slash and burn.
8. Contract duration commitment.
9. The type of wood (dense and strong or light and less strong).
10. The quality of the wood type (even the same wood type has variable quality).
11. The type, size and structure of the nails (you would not believe the variability and diversity of something as apparently simple as a nail).
12. Delivery volumes.
13. Delivery frequency.
14. Number of delivery locations (dispersed or one central point).
15. Transportation costs.
16. Penalties for consequential loss due to late delivery or product failure.

17. Supplier or customer-managed inventory.

18. Currency in which payment is to be made (currency fluctuations play a part).

19. Does it have to be wood – what about alternative materials?

20. Sole supply or multiple suppliers.

21. Payment terms.

22. Returns policy.

23. Quality of customer service.

24. Quality of the relationship between buyer and seller.

Plus, all of the additional ones that you thought of that are not listed above, and which now probably take the list close to 40 variables.

INSIGHTS AND LEARNING

Think broad and deep.

Often the first thing we think about in a negotiation is 'price'; how much are they asking, how much will I pay, how much is it worth, how much can I sell it for, what's the minimum I am prepared to sell it for?

Price is important, but it is not always the most important thing. Imagine if Linhua was able to source incredibly cheap pallets, but as soon as they had their cargo stacked on top and were loaded on to the truck the pallets collapsed and thousands of Renminbi (RMB) of product were destroyed with each attempted lift.

Is price still the most important variable? Clearly not, as the saving of a few RMB per pallet would potentially cost the loss of thousands of RMB in a matter of seconds. It's not good negotiation sense, it's not good business sense… it's nonsense.

So, put price at the top of the list if you must, but think broad and deep – think 'What else is important here?'

HOW CAN I USE THIS?

For a current negotiation, make a list of all of the variables that you think are relevant.

Now try to double it.

If you're an 'average' negotiator, then it's normal to miss lots of relevant variables.

In an exercise at a recent negotiation workshop, a group was challenged to come up with a list of at least 20 different variables that applied to a typical negotiation case study. After just 15 minutes they had compiled a list of 35. How many did you come up with just now?

This simple exercise illustrates:

1. How many variables are involved in just one negotiation.
2. How many variables are simply not considered, perhaps due to a perceived lack of time or a feeling that five or six variables is enough to deal with.

In any negotiation, the more variables you have to play with, the more options you have, and the greater the chance of finding an acceptable agreement.

Variables can be continuous, such as price or time, or they can change in discrete steps, for example an item is included in the deal or it is not, half of it is, etc.

Variables also have multiple dimensions. For example, when talking about price, it's not just about the amount; other variables include the time taken to pay and how it is paid (cash, credit or trading for something else).

To identify negotiation variables, ask, *'What are the things that are important to me and to the other party in this situation?'*

From a simple situation involving pieces of wood and nails, Linhua uncovered 24.

If you're involved in more complex negotiations, then maybe you're dealing with closer to 40 or 50 variables.

Once you've made your list it's important to prioritise the variables and, where possible, attach a 'value' to each.

45 POWERLESS TO NEGOTIATE

45 POWERLESS TO NEGOTIATE

Tim was trying to get to work.

Tim is the Sales Director for a large, international organisation, and he's worried that he might be late for the monthly board meeting.

There had been heavy snowfall overnight and, as he lived near the bottom of a hill, he had seen from his window several vehicles struggling to get up the hill that morning.

He had watched some cars slide back down the hill and their owners had abandoned their car at the side of the road in a flat section, out of the way. Some had made it to the top, but with considerable difficulty and risk.

Tim had no choice, he had to get to work and there was no way to avoid the hill.

Five minutes later Tim waited at the bottom of the slope, with his engine running, he watched as a driver in front attempted to get to the top.

The driver was obviously struggling, though he was making some steady, if faltering, progress.

Tim knew that he should not try to get up the hill directly behind the driver in front. He imagined a situation where the car in front came to a halt, and even started slipping back down the hill into his car, so he decided to wait until the driver was at least 70% of the way up the hill. His strategy was to then approach at a steady speed, hoping to maintain sufficient momentum to propel him to the top without stopping.

As the other car got near the top Tim set off, with gritted teeth, eyes peeled wide and white knuckles.

To Tim's horror, he saw the car in front halt, about 30 feet from the top, and so Tim too was forced to stop, a safe distance behind the vehicle. To his relief, he then saw two youths, probably about 16 or 17 years old, approach the driver in front, speak to him through the car window, and then proceed to push his car to the top of the hill.

Great, thought Tim. If those guys are prepared to help me too, I just might get to my meeting in time.

Sure enough, once the first driver had been pushed to the top, and disappeared from view, the youths approached Tim and asked him if he would like a push up the hill.

Tim:	'That would be great lads, as I don't know what else to do, stuck here halfway up the hill.'
Youth 1:	'Happy to help – that will be £10 please.'
Tim:	'What, £10 for a 30-second push? You're joking aren't you?'
Youth 1:	'Well that's what the guy in front gave us, and he seemed to think it a fair price to get him out of a predicament.'
Tim:	'Come on lads, £10 pound's a bit steep.'
Youth 1:	'Not as steep as this hill, sir.'
Tim:	'I'll tell you what, I'll give you £5 to get me to the top.'
Youth 2:	(Leaning forward to the driver's window) 'Sir, as I see it, you're in no position to negotiate.'

INSIGHTS AND LEARNING

This small incident has a number of strong negotiation messages.

It illustrates:

- The 'power balance' between two parties.
- The person with the greatest need is in a weaker position.
- When circumstances dictate, one party can charge a lot more for something than under normal conditions – that's why the umbrella sales people come out on to the city streets when it's raining. You don't see them when the sun is shining, and it's why they can charge £10 for a £2 umbrella.
- How a person who is normally used to being in control, and holding a powerful position in negotiations (remember he's the Sales Director of a major corporation), can find himself in an unfamiliar and disempowering negotiation position.
- How the lack of a BATNA ('Best Alternative To a Negotiated Agreement') meant that Tim had little option other than to either try to negotiate a better price or to agree to their demand for £10.
- The effect that time pressure can have in the negotiation as it often means that the person who is under most time pressure (Tim in this case) is likely to concede quickly and to yield more.
- How price and value are not the same thing.

Time gave them the £10 they asked for, he was over the hill within 30 seconds and he arrived just in time for the start of the board meeting.

HOW CAN I USE THIS?

Consider each of the insights and lessons above and, whilst you can never predict a situation you might find yourself in, at least try to relate these important negotiation principles to your own business and personal life.

When have you needed something urgently or desperately, and what have been the consequences for you in terms of the power balance between you and the other party?

Have you made the mistake of admitting to needing to close a deal quickly or, even if not verbally, could you have conveyed your agitation non-verbally, through your body language or the speed with which you tried to move things along?

More positively, have you paid more for something than you normally would, but thinking objectively about it you're happy to have done so because, relative to the opportunity loss or consequential damage that would have resulted from not doing the deal, you made a sensible decision?

Remember that having a powerful job, perhaps one in which you're used to leveraging the power of your position and authority, can be irrelevant when you find yourself in very different circumstances. The Chief Executive in the lifeboat is no different from all of the other random passengers crammed into the dinghy adrift at sea.

I am reminded of a story of a famous person checking in for a flight and asking if she could be upgraded. The check-in assistant said that would not be possible, to which the celebrity challenged the check-in assistant with, *'Do you know who I am?'* *'One moment, madam,'* said the check-in assistant, at which point she picked up the airport public address system and announced, *'Can I please request a supervisor to desk 14? I have a passenger here who does not know who she is.'*

That story, unlike the cases in this book, is probably not true, but it is nevertheless funny, and a good example of how excessive hubris can backfire.

It has been emphasised elsewhere in this book that you must have a BATNA. If you don't, your power is wiped out, you lose confidence, you might have to resort to bluff, and your negotiating position is massively reduced. If you do not have a BATNA, put all of your energy into finding or creating one before you go into the negotiation.

SEQUEL

Two years later, Tim's organisation decided to grow the size of the sales team at his head office, where he worked.

They recruited four new sales people to join as junior members of the team. One of whom was called Craig.

He lived at the top of the hill.

46 ZOPA

46 ZOPA

Holiday coach driver, speaking to the owner of an independent hotel, in reception at 9:30pm.

'Hi, I have a party of 34 people in a coach a few hundred yards down the road. The coach has broken down and there's no chance of getting it repaired tonight. I wondered if you had enough rooms to accommodate my party. They're all couples, so we need 16 rooms plus one for me – or I can sleep on the coach. We don't need any food tonight as everyone has already had dinner at a restaurant.'

Imagine you're the owner of the hotel. You have 20 rooms available and you're very unlikely to get any other walk-in customers that night. The restaurant has closed, but you will be able to provide a full breakfast the next morning for which you would charge the standard €15 per person.

In this case, assume everyone will pay €15 for breakfast, and assume that it costs you €5 to service each room per day. Your standard walk-in room rate is €70 per room for up to two people.

What would you offer as the room rate, and what is the minimum you would be prepared to agree to?

Think about this carefully before you read further. How much would you ask per room?

Now consider whether your response would be different if you were not the hotel manager, but were instead the evening receptionist working a shift that ends at 12:00 midnight. Your manager has the night off so is not on the premises.

Now imagine you're the coach driver and, incidentally, the owner of the holiday business. What is the maximum you would be prepared to pay per room, and what is the minimum you would like to get the price down to?

What if you were one of the passengers on the coach?

INSIGHTS AND LEARNING

Perhaps the surprising, or even astounding, point of this case is that the hotel manager offered the 17 rooms for just €10 each, on the understanding that he also charged each person for the €15 breakfast, which of course most would take in any case.

He knew that he would earn 34 x €15 for the breakfasts, minus the cost of the breakfasts (just €3 each), which gives a net profit of €408, minus the cost of servicing 17 rooms (€85). Add in 17 rooms at €10 and, overall, his net gain would be €500.

This is not a lot of money, but it's €500 of profit that goes directly to his bottom line, and this does not take into account the bar takings that would almost certainly be made from a coach load of weary travellers, which at even a modest €5 per person, plus a very thirsty coach driver, would mean his profit could be closer to €700.

This is €700 net profit that he did not have two minutes previously.

The hotel manager could of course point to the tariff board and say, *'Well, we do have rooms available, and they're €70 per night per couple.'* That's around €1,200 revenue, but is it really reasonable to expect to get the full price for so many rooms so late in the evening? The coach driver knows the rooms are almost certainly not going to be sold to anyone else, and as the clock ticks the opportunity for the hotel manager to earn revenue from the rooms evaporates.

There are of course many other options, such as offering a €20 discount on each room, giving the coach driver a room for free, offering a 'free' breakfast for each guest, offering to keep the bar open later than normal…

The coach driver could also suggest that everyone sleeps on the bus and he gives each person a €40 refund, which is €30 less than he would have to pay to the hotel if the hotel manager stuck to his published rate.

This calculation is simple economics, but not so simple when you're faced with a difficult situation such as this where paying customers are involved and you have a reputation to uphold. Would you really make your customers sleep on the coach?

Getting back to the hotel manager… if you were in his position, how would you feel about giving the rooms away for free, just so long as you charged for 35 breakfasts?

Most people would consider that bad business, but ask yourself this question… if it were a case of giving the rooms away for free and making a clear profit of €383, or the coach driver walking away and you getting no profit whatsoever, which would you choose then?

If you were the night receptionist, then things might be considerably different. You don't make the profit, it's not your hotel and probably, more than anything, the very last thing you need at 9:30 in the evening is to receive 34 weary passengers and a coach driver, keep the bar open, be run off your feet and miss the snooker match that you're secretly watching on your television behind the reception desk.

If you were the coach driver, you may be prepared to pay 70% of the normal price, and a less flexible hotel manager might want at least 50%. Even in this case, there is a ZOPA, a zone of potential agreement, and so a deal is perfectly possible. The coach driver is prepared to pay €49 per room and the manager is prepared to let them go for €35 each – quite a comfortable area for agreement, provided they can negotiate themselves into that zone.

HOW CAN I USE THIS?

If no ZOPA exists between two parties, then it's unlikely, though not impossible, that an agreement can be made.

Imagine, for example, that in a car sale the only variable is price; the seller is not willing to sell for less than €10,000, and the buyer is not willing to pay more than €9,000, then a deal does not appear to be possible; a state of stalemate exists.

In contrast, in the car sale case below a deal is possible, as the seller's minimum price is below the maximum the buyer is prepared to pay.

However, and as starkly illustrated in case **44** – 'Value Discovery', in most negotiations there are far more variables involved, and so a deal may be possible where no ZOPA appears to exist for one particular variable.

The seller may be prepared to accept less if the buyer were to pay in cash on the spot, allow the seller to remove the CD interchanger unit, and to cash in the value of the remaining vehicle excise duty (road tax). The buyer may be prepared to pay more if the seller were to fit the car with new tyres, allow staged payments over a six-month period or replace the scratched wing mirror and deliver the car to them.

Successful negotiators deal with multiple variables simultaneously, and they make trades between them. It can take time but it's worth it. The eventual deal results in an effective 'configuration of agreements' within ZOPAs for multiple variables.

But what if no ZOPA exists? Well, there are still things that can be done:

- One or both parties will need to exercise their BATNA (see case 20 and Part Two), effectively 'walking away' to an alternative (different) solution.

- One of the parties realises, or is persuaded by the other, that their BATNA is not as good as they first thought, and they therefore accept the best deal they can get.

- One party was pretending to have a BATNA, and is now stuck; they either accept the deal or walk away to a much worse situation! – recall what happened to Ron in case 33 – 'Bluff'.

- One person changes their max/min threshold; their 'walk away point'.

- One or both parties have been lying about their ZOPA; they're both now stuck!

- Both parties decide to 'split the difference' in the interests of clinching a deal on the basis that a 'half win' for each of them is better than no deal at all.

47 YOU'LL HAVE TO DO BETTER

47 YOU'LL HAVE TO DO BETTER

Hayley: (Insurance representative.) *'Thanks for calling Reliable Insurance. My name's Hayley. How may I help you?'*

Patrick: *'Hi Hayley, thanks for taking my call. I'm confused. I've just had my insurance renewal quote and, despite not making any claims and my car being a year older, the premium you're quoting is £490, which is 19% higher than last year. I'm at a loss to understand why you're charging me a massive increase in annual cost, when I'm a safe driver, I have never had a car accident in my life and my car is worth about £2,000 less than it was this time last year.'*

Hayley: *'I'm sorry to hear that Mr Crawford, but the premiums are calculated automatically and I think you will find that insurance premiums generally have gone up over the past year due to a rise in claims. As you've taken the trouble to contact us today, I can give you a reduction in the renewal quote over the phone, which would bring your insurance down to £453 which is just 10% more than last year.'*

Patrick: *'I understand the effects of market dynamics, but in just 25 minutes I've found comparable cover for far less. You will have to do better than that.'*

Hayley: *'What have you been quoted, sir?'*

Patrick: *'I'm looking at four quotes here, one of which is almost the same as yours, but the other three are lower – one of them considerably so.'*

Hayley: *'Can you please give me the figures and the names of the companies that have given you the quotes?'*

Patrick gave honest information, quoting the companies and their proposed insurance quotes. (Note: it would have been foolish to try to lie at this point as the insurers have their own software, which enables them to compare the market instantly.)

Hayley: *'Mr Crawford, I see your point. However, some of the companies you're quoting are not necessarily offering exactly the same as our policy. For example, company 3 does not offer the replacement vehicle option that you currently have with us, and company 4, whilst it looks very cheap, is a brand new player in the market without a track record. Of course it's your choice, but I wouldn't insure my car with a company I've never heard of. As I said, I can reduce the premium increase to just 10% of last year's premium.'*

Patrick:	'And as I said previously, you'll have to do better than that.'
Hayley:	'Mr Crawford, how much better would I have to do?'
Patrick:	'Hayley, I'm reasonable guy, and I'm not asking you to match the lowest quote. I also accept that company 3 does not exactly provide what you're offering in terms of a replacement vehicle, but company 2 does So, if you're prepared to match the quote of company 2, which is £392, just £20 less than what I paid you last year, then I will renew with you now and that can be the end of this conversation.'.
Hayley:	'Mr Crawford, can you please give me a moment to check in with my supervisor?'

...

'Mr Crawford, I've spoken with my supervisor and I'm really sorry but there is no way that we can match the quote of company 2. However, what I have managed to secure from her is an agreement to hold your premium at last year's rate. I recognise that company 2 are £20 cheaper, but she and I really have tried our best to get the premium as low as possible. I hope you feel able to accept the flat premium and, at the same time, avoid any break in your cover or the hassle of trying to change insurers. At the same time, I appreciate that £20 is £20 and so if you feel you do need to leave us, then I would be sorry, but I would understand and I would respect your decision.'

Ninety seconds later Patrick put the phone down having secured another year's insurance at last year's premium. Despite not getting a reduction in last year's premium, he was still very happy, as is explained below.

INSIGHTS AND LEARNING

Saying to the other party, 'You'll have to do better' does not say exactly how much better they should do. In this sense, it puts the responsibility on to them to make a concession of their choosing and magnitude – in this case price was the most important variable.

With just five words and 10 seconds Patrick achieved a first round cost saving of £37.

Repeating those same five words a few seconds later saved him a further £41, reducing the proposed premium back to the previous year's level.

Patrick was pleased that just by asking, holding out and not accepting the first offer (written) or second (verbal), he saved £78. The money was important to Patrick, but not as important as his sense of achievement in practising his negotiation skills and achieving a win as a result – at a price he was very happy to pay.

Patrick also felt that he had genuinely pushed Hayley and her supervisor as far as was reasonable. Sure, he could have asked to speak to the supervisor's supervisor, but that may not have yielded any further concession; it would have taken longer and may have ended in bad feelings. The fact that Hayley ended her final offer by saying that she understood if Patrick still felt the need to go to another insurer signalled to him that she was at her 'walk-away point'.

Patrick's real target was to keep his premium the same as last year. He was using company 2 as a stretch target so, again, he was happy with the result.

The insurance company retained a loyal customer for another year – one who's a safe driver so unlikely to cause a loss. Their problem will be in 12 months' time when Patrick, is faced with another increase and will have learned to use the same technique again.

Apart from negotiating over price and maintaining the contract or tearing it up, other variables might have been brought into the equation, such as Hayley guaranteeing a fixed premium for the next two years, giving a further discount (above normal) on motoring breakdown insurance or throwing in free legal cover. The latter two items generally have more value to the customer than they cost the provider, which illustrates that price is not the same as value (see case 17 – 'Good, Cheap, Fast'). Patrick might also have thought about re-insuring his wife's car with Hayley – something that he did not think about at the time.

Other important lessons that we can take from this simple phone negotiation are Patrick's use of competitive benchmark data and Hayley's challenge for him to provide such data – again, a smart move. However, this case is about *'You'll have to do better'*, so let's dig a bit deeper into that.

HOW CAN I USE THIS?

How you can use this is self-explanatory. However, what do you do if it is used on you?

You might hear, *'You'll have to do better than that'* expressed in other ways, such as *'I'm sorry, but that just won't cut it', 'It's not good enough', 'I cannot accept that'* or similar.

Of course, the big unanswered question in this statement is *'Exactly how much better do I have to do?'* Hayley was smart enough to ask this the second time around.

You might think that responding in this way puts Hayley in a weak position, because the other person could ask for a ridiculous price reduction or make some other outrageous request. However, Hayley in that case could use a range of tactics in response, such as flinching (see explanation in Part Two), laughing politely, saying *'No way can I do that – it's totally out of the ballpark'*, walking away, proposing that they both end the negotiation as it is unlikely to go anywhere or proposing a much more reasonable counter offer. In fact, the requester risks making themselves look like a fool or someone out of touch with the market for making such a ridiculous request.

At least when you ask, *'Exactly how much better do I have to do?'* you put the pressure back on the other party to respond with a specific number, request or whatever.

The 'do much better' tactic is most often used by purchasers, though not always. A seller may be in a position of power, perhaps because they possess something that is in short supply, is in great demand, or for which the purchaser has up until now made a mediocre offer.

So, if this is used on you:

- Ask, *'Exactly how much better do I have to do?'*

- Do not be pressurised into giving a new proposal that is 'better' without the other party answering this question first; after all, you've made your proposal so the ball is now in their court to make a counter proposal.

- Ask, *'So, exactly what would you be prepared to agree to?'* Again, get them to be specific and to lay down a 'marker' (see case 38 – 'Laying Down a Marker').

- Say, *'I appreciate that you are not happy with what I have proposed, so can you please be specific about which aspects of my proposal you ARE happy with, so we can tick these off, and which we need to discuss further?'* This creates a sense of progression on some items, and isolates those that are still in contention.

- Say, *'I'm sorry to hear that, but this is my final offer; so unless we can reconfigure some of the other variables, then I don't know how we can reach an agreement; if you're not happy with X, then where else do you have flexibility to move to enable me to move on X? Come on... a negotiation requires movement on both sides.'*

- Say, *'[name of person], neither of us have the time to play negotiation games, give me YOUR best offer and we can then flush out a deal – this is taking far too long.'*

Note, you may have noticed some similarity with case 19 – 'Onus Transfer'. They are different cases that illustrate different negotiation dimensions. However, this does show the inter-connectedness of strategies and tactics, and dynamics of what goes on, at multiple levels, in negotiations.

48 CORRUPTION AND BRIBERY

48 CORRUPTION AND BRIBERY

Tommaso Battaglia – an Italian businessman, on a temporary assignment in Munich, was speaking with Andreas Schmidt, a senior German official via telephone.

Tommaso: *'Hello Mr Schmidt, it's Tommaso Battaglia here from Plicasso Sunglasses. I am told that you're responsible for overseeing the management of the Reichlich shopping mall where we're installing our retail designer outlet. Is that correct?'*

Andreas: *'Hello Mr Battaglia, yes, that is correct. How may I help you?'*

Tommaso: *'Mr Schmidt, we're due to finalise the shop fitting work in six days' time, with a view to opening the store seven days from now. There seems to be an issue that we had not foreseen; we're being told by the shopping centre administrator that it could take anything between three and six weeks to get a phone line installed into the shop.'*

Andreas: *'Yes, that doesn't surprise me; it can take that long.'*

Tommaso: *'But surely that's ridiculous. Back in Italy, where we've opened numerous shops, we've either taken over a previous retail shop which has a phone line already connected or, if it's new premises, the latest we've had to wait was just three days. We have to open on the 17th, and without a phone line we can't connect our point of sale equipment, access the internet or make and receive phone calls. It simply will not be possible to do business without such a connection.'*

Andreas: *'Are you at the shop now?'*

Tommaso: *'Yes – I will be here for the next few hours.'*

Andreas: *'I will come down to see you within the hour.'*

One hour later…

Andreas: *'Mr Battaglia – I see your predicament. These things take time but, if you're prepared to give what I believe you Italians call a little "bustarella"*, then I could help you to obtain the phone line more quickly.'*

Tommaso: (Slightly taken aback.) *'That's totally weird. I really don't get it. Who's the German and who's the Italian in this situation?!'*

---

*   An envelope containing cash.

SEQUEL, AND TWIST IN THE TALE

Tommaso gave Mr Schmidt the money and he got his phone line within three days. The shop opened on time and benefitted from a healthy first day's trading.

Andreas Schmidt was not only German, a nationality not so readily associated with corruption than other countries, including Italy, he was also a retired judge.

INSIGHTS AND LEARNING

Corruption exists. Corruption is endemic and if you don't believe it, just open any national/international newspaper or listen to the news, where you will see a massive amount of corruption across all areas of business, economic and political life. In some societies corruption is a way of life – it's the norm.

This case is a mild example of petty corruption – oiling the palms of an official in order to get something, or obtain it quicker than going through the normal channels. It involved only a few hundred Euros and Tommaso, whilst not happy with having to pay a bribe, knew that the cost of not getting his phone line in time would far outweigh the contents of the envelope.

Whilst egregious large-scale corruption is detestable, a self-serving bias is partly understandable. Who doesn't want the very best for themselves, their friends and relatives? If you doubt this, ask yourself whom you vote for and why? Chances are it's because that candidate is proposing policies and actions that are going to benefit you and those close to you.

Now, voting is not corruption, it's supposed to be the very opposite – fair and democratic. However, many voting systems are themselves riddled with corruption. The point here is that when put under pressure, or when presented with an easy opportunity, people will often look after themselves first.

But what do you do when faced with someone from the other side who is corrupt?

HOW CAN I USE THIS?

Start with yourself:

1. Obey the law and encourage others around you to do the same.
2. Neither pay nor accept bribes.
3. If you run or work for a business, develop or encourage the creation of anti-corruption policies and guidelines – a written code of conduct.
4. Education and training for all employees about corruption and how to avoid or report it should be part of any organisation's induction programme.

5. Establish internal whistle-blowing hotlines and internal audit procedures.

6. Ensure that significant deals involve a number of parties from both sides, to minimise the risk of two individuals colluding between themselves.

If you suspect a personal agenda from another party, get the feeling that you're being asked to 'oil the wheels', or are even directly asked for a favour, be it monetary or something else, then there are a number of things you can do. We start with options that we do not necessarily recommend, but which are, nevertheless, options:

1. Just accept that unless you comply there is no way that you will make progress, and do what they say. When I was trying to get into the Lagos airport departure terminal to fly home, a soldier dressed in camouflage and carrying an AK47 stepped in front of me. *'Something for the boys?'* enquired the soldier, with a smile on his face. It was easier to give him $5 than risk a confrontation and no doubt further blocks to progress through a foreign airport. When people are armed with guns it's probably best to take the easier option. In business, if you do not comply, then you may find that 'complications' arise, delays, safety notices, customs officials holding deliveries in quarantine, and a whole string of minor inconveniences that quickly turn into major delays and rejections.

2. Negotiate a 'settlement' that gives them part of what they're asking for, but without this being excessive or damaging to your own position. Tommaso did hand over some cash, but he negotiated with Andreas a more reasonable figure and still got what he needed.

3. Anticipate these problems and plan for inconveniences and delays. If you're expecting such things, then manage it in a way to avoid creating situations where you can fall prey to retaliation. It may be as simple as building in a 100% time buffer because if you're desperate, and/or show that desperation, then the risk of you caving in to unethical demands will increase.

4. Quote your company policy and values, stating that this is not the way you do business. You're strictly prohibited from engaging in any practices that are not ethical or which do not comply with your company's Code of Conduct.

5. Internally communicate incidents when demands are rejected, and develop a consistent approach to dealing with bribery issues. Senior managers and compliance officers can spread the word in how the company is fighting back against bribery. Such communications show how the organisation is walking its talk in terms of fighting bribery and corruption issues.

6. Consider externally reporting serious attempts of bribery to the authorities or to the press, or threaten to do so if such requests continue.

7. Set up a working party to investigate and report back on an issue. Be bound

by the decision and if an individual keeps pushing for an alternative course of action, which does not make sense in light of the working party's findings, you can say the matter has been properly investigated and a decision made so it's not appropriate to keep bringing the matter up.

8. Use 'arms' length' technologies to try to create distance between negotiating parties; for example, using e-bidding, e-auctions, a clear level playing field, greater efficiency and transparent bidding process and the like.

9. Insist that for any particular direction to be pursued there need to be at least two people from your side who support it.

49 RED HERRING

49 RED HERRING

A businessman and his colleague were travelling on a company-funded overnight flight from New York to London. They often travelled in business class, but since the global recession hit they now have to travel in economy/coach class. To add to their annoyance, they found they were sitting next to two young excitable girls.

The girls, aged 20 and 21, had flown before but only very occasionally, and always within the US – never long haul and never without their parents. Understandably, this was an adventure of a lifetime for them. They were talking excitedly to each other.

Whilst the plane was preparing for takeoff the businessman called over one of the stewardesses. Quite openly, within earshot of the two girls, he complained that he and his colleague could not remain in these seats as they wanted some peace and quiet during the night flight. He asked if it would be possible for them to move to a quieter cabin.

The stewardess said that she would see what she could do. She said that as the flight was not fully booked there may be a possibility, but there were no guarantees.

The businessman and his colleague sat back and waited, hoping that they might get an upgrade to business class, or at least to premium economy, especially as the stewardess had said that the flight was not full. He and his colleague were used to the additional space, quiet, enhanced service and extra attention that such cabins have provided them in the past, and to hear that the flight was not full should mean that there were spare seats in the higher end cabins – why let them go to waste?

After a few minutes the Stewardess returned and said that, unfortunately, it would not be possible to move them.

At this point the businessman became agitated and annoyed, saying, *'You just told us that the flight is not full, so there must be some seats up front that are not being used – we're only talking about two seats.'*

Stewardess: *'I understand your position, sir. The only thing I can do is to speak to the captain as he has the final say in such matters.'*

Three minutes later the captain came to see the businessman and his colleague.

Captain: *'Sir, I understand that you're not happy with your seating arrangement. I am happy to say that we have found two seats in business class…'*

(Turning to the two girls) *'Ladies, would you like to accompany me to the business class section so these two gentlemen can get some sleep?'*

INSIGHTS AND LEARNING

Touché!

On the surface of the situation the businessman got what he wanted, which was not to be disturbed any further by the excitable girls. He had asked if they could be moved.

Well, he got what he wanted because 'they' (the girls) were moved!

This is a good example of one party trying to use a 'red herring' (needing to be away from the girls) as an excuse to get what they really wanted, which was to be upgraded. See below, and Part Two, for a definition of 'Red Herring'.

In fact, the captain took the businessman at his word, i.e. he and his colleague wanted to be seated away from the girls, and, as a consequence, the girls moved from a state of excitement, to elation to ecstasy. The only condition the captain imposed was that by placing the young ladies in business class he expected them to fully enjoy the experience in a less excitable and more dignified manner. Of course, they gladly complied. They were screaming with delight inside but talked quietly on the outside, and they 'dined out' on the story for several years.

So did the captain. Of course he was smart, but he deliberately played dumb, and took considerable pleasure from 'resolving' the situation in a rather clever way.

The two girls were also happy not to be sitting next to two rude, boring old businessmen who would probably snore through the overnight flight anyway – if they could get any sleep that is!

HOW CAN I USE THIS?

In three ways…

Firstly, be careful of pushing too hard for something; it can backfire, confound the achievement of your goals or, even worse, act against you in favour of another party – that's a double negative hit for you.

Sometimes by pushing too hard you defeat your objective. It's a bit like trying too hard to impress someone or appearing too needy. The most likely response in these situations is to not be impressed, to want to run away or… to call the police.

Secondly, and which is the theme of this case, be careful of using what in negotiation terms is called a 'red herring' – pretending you want something else in order to get what you really want.

The term is supposed to originate in the use of a kipper (a strong-smelling smoked fish) to train hounds to follow a scent when hunting, or to divert them off the trail.

A buyer may focus attention on a minor issue in order to get her way on a major one. For example, she might suggest that her reason for not being able to agree to 'X' is because of 'Y'. She gives in later, on the condition that you provide 'Z'. The point is that 'Y' was never an issue for her in the first place; it was a red herring.

As a diversionary tactic, the red herring can:

- Deflect attention from what you're really interested in, towards something else.

- Be used to cause the other party to waste time chasing things they do not need to and, in doing so, they run short of time to pursue other matters.

- Prevent the other party from discovering or questioning you about something you would rather they did not.

- Enable you to obtain a much bigger concession on the thing that is really of interest to you.

The red herring is a particularly devious tactic.

To deal with a suspected red herring:

- Question the reasons behind the other party's stance; this may well expose a weakness in their argument.

- Ask the other party why this particular request is so important, and whether it is more important than other matters; this may help you to flush out whether it is real or fake.

- Use the red herring yourself by calling their bluff. For example, make out that it's difficult for you to do something the other party is requesting, but promise to try to get it approved or included in the deal if the other party agrees to something else that you want.

- Use it when you *are* able to honour a request, but when you want to imply that you're doing them a big favour. In doing so, make them aware that you're really making a big step towards them by honouring this request and you will be looking for some form of reciprocity from them as part of the deal, or in the near future. See case 27 – 'Reciprocity', and section Two for more information.

- If it really is not such an important issue for the other party (discovered as a result of one or more of the above tactics), they may prefer you to spend your time and energy working on the issues that really are important to them rather than give away favours on something that they do not really want or need.

- Remember, whenever you're asked for something, a suspected red herring or not, and it's easy for you to meet the request, never give it away easily; use the opportunity to highlight the value of this particular concession, what it will 'cost' you, and ask for something in return.

Finally, when you get annoyed with people, especially when you think they're in a lower position than you – such as the self-important businessman's view of airline cabin crew or his fellow passengers, or the pompous lady mentioned in case 45, trying to check-in for her flight, be careful. People have different sources and degrees of power. Even if they're not empowered to grant certain concessions, in this case a cabin upgrade, they can be obstinate blocks to your progress and achievement of your ambitions.

In negotiation terms they're called 'gatekeepers' or 'blockers'. They have relatively less power than more senior people, but they do have the power to enable or disable your progress in a few critical ways or channels.

Consider, for example, the medical secretary who either grants the pharmaceutical representative a meeting with the consultant or who says that, unfortunately, the consultant's diary is fully booked before then going on holiday, and in any case she rarely sees medical representatives. Compare this with the same person who says, *'Actually, I'm not really supposed to do this, but I know she has a free 20 minutes right now – let me see if I can get you in to see her for a quick conversation.'*

Even if the other party does have the empowerment to grant a concession, if you've annoyed or irritated them, the chances are they'll try to confound you and be laughing all the way home.

They'll be the ones dining out on the story for years to come, whilst you continue to stew in your own self-cooked juice.

Hopefully the businessman learned a lesson from this case too.

50 WHEN IN ROME – OR ATHENS

50 WHEN IN ROME – OR ATHENS

When he was in his late 20's, David, from the UK, had the opportunity to travel to Greece as a junior project manager, working alongside Helga, a far more experienced project leader from Berlin. They were on a 3-day business trip to negotiate the renewal of a contract. Neither David nor Helga had been to Greece before and they had inherited the project from two of their colleagues just a few weeks previously.

The meeting with the Greek counterparties was scheduled to start at 09:00.

At 09:05 Helga was becoming visibly agitated by the fact that not a single person from the Greek host company had arrived in the meeting room.

At 09:10 she instructed David to go to reception to find out what was happening, and where everyone was. David returned five minutes later to find Helga, still on her own, but now out of her seat and pacing up and down.

David assured her that he had been told that some people would be along shortly, but by 09:18 Helga was totally losing her cool, pacing up and down, raising her voice at David, who by now was feeling awkward and uncomfortable.

At 09:24 Spiros sauntered into the room, smiling and sipping his ice-cool Frappe coffee.

Within seconds, his smile was wiped off his face as he was confronted with an extremely assertive German lady, whose first words to him were, 'And where on Earth have you been? Where are all the others?' Spiros was stunned. He thought he was early!

Suffice to say, the negotiation did not go well. It took several hours for Helga to rebuild some semblance of rapport with the Greeks, and whilst the contract was eventually renegotiated, Helga was never invited back to the Greek subsidiary again.

INSIGHTS AND LEARNING

To all involved, this incident was a powerful lesson in how cultural expectations can collide, and how serious consequences can arise when insufficient knowledge, care and allowances are made for the cultural norms around expected or anticipated behaviours of the other party.

If Helga, or David for that matter, had taken the time to consider the culture they were visiting before they did their planning or stepped on the plane, then this awkward incident could easily have been avoided. The visitors could have requested an earlier start time to the meeting, anticipating that the Greeks would most likely not be 'on time'. Then, expecting them to be 'late', the visitors could have arranged a more fluid agenda, relaxed and gone with the flow.

In fairness, whilst Helga allowed what she perceived as late, inconsiderate and bordering on rude behaviour to affect her own attitude and behaviour, cultural awareness, understanding and tolerance should be a two-way street. The Greeks, knowing that they were being visited by a German and a British person, should have been aware that those two cultures have different viewpoints of what punctuality and timeliness mean.

HOW CAN I USE THIS?

This is just one example of how difficulties can arise when cultures have different expectations of what should and should not happen. There are countless others, some of which have been graphically recounted in this book.

In this example, the cultural dimension is one of punctuality and respect for the time of others. So, when planning your negotiations, regardless of culture, build in buffer time, expect and plan for delays and never ever show any signs of a need for urgency. In any negotiation, the person under the most time pressure has less power. Feeling pressured to agree a deal means you're more likely to concede more, concede quickly and leave money on the table.

The party with more time to spare, less urgency and no fixed deadline is likely to be more relaxed about the negotiation, and may even watch in mild amusement as the other party fidgets, tries to push things along a lot quicker or shows signs of needing a deal and needing it today.

Never appear too desperate to get the deal – even when you are!

51 HOSTAGE

51 HOSTAGE

Important note:

This traumatic case ends happily. It's important to state this before you read further.

'Happily' in so much as any kidnapping and hostage situation can be said to do so. At least no person was harmed during the process and, afterwards, the freed hostage felt able to talk about the experience without feeling lasting psychological damage – remarkable!

Emilié, from Belgium, was cycling with two American friends in South America. It was day six of a 12-day holiday.

Was she wise to be doing so? Maybe not, particularly with the troubles in that part of the world, but she was with two close friends, one male and one female, and so she felt some degree of security. In any case, Emilié was, by nature, an adventurer and risk-taker; she liked to live on the edge.

Cycling up a long hill was taking its toll, but Emilié was fit and healthy. Having engaged in some light-hearted banter with her friends as they huffed up the hill, Emilié decided to push ahead a bit harder and get to the top first.

Five minutes later her American friends found her bicycle at the side of the road – with no sign of Emilié.

An armed gang, who had heard the 'American' voices of her friends, had assumed that Emilié was also American and had swiftly captured her. They had dragged her into the forest within seconds, leaving her bicycle at the side of the road. No trace was left of their path.

We now know that Emilié was kept in a small wooden hut, in the depths of the forest, for five days. Terrified and incapable of escaping, this was, of course, her worst nightmare.

After five days Emilié was released, unharmed, at the side of a quiet road in a different area; her captors gave her a litre of water, a blanket and a bar of chocolate. A passing motorist who saw her desperation quickly rescued her and took her to a small hospital in the nearest town.

Emilié is now safe and well. She was not ill-treated during those terrifying five days, but she did learn some valuable negotiation lessons throughout the process. Lessons she's keen to pass on to you, the reader.

INSIGHTS AND LEARNING

Where does one begin with this case? One would prefer it to have never happened but it did. So what can we learn about negotiating in extreme circumstances?

Having survived the first 48 hours in pure fear, anger and a sense of not being able to do anything, Emilié managed to start thinking more clearly. What she really wanted to do was to understand who the 'boss' was, and then to try to talk to that person directly.

She reckoned that if she could get to the 'boss', then that would be the smartest move, as all of the other rebels would then fall in line and take their lead. She needed to understand why she had been kidnapped, what the rebels hoped to achieve and what, if anything, they needed from her.

She also wanted to use whatever negotiation levers she could and, whilst appearing to be in a powerless situation, she thought long and hard about what she could say or do that might tip the power balance a little more in her direction.

When the kidnappers found that Emilié had a Belgian passport, they did not know what to do with her. However, she was probably still valuable to them, possibly as a 'bargaining card', and so they weren't going to give her up easily. Emilié believes that the way in which she communicated and negotiated with the rebels over those five days saved her life.

So, what exactly did she do to persuade the leader of the rebels to release her?

She observed that the rebel group appeared nervous; that their camp was temporary and they were extremely vigilant. She noted that whilst she was kept in a secure, wooden cabin, she was not bound or gagged and was free to move around. She interpreted their nervousness and temporary location as a sign that things could change quickly. The fact that she had not been gagged implied to Emilié that they were not likely to be extremely cruel, and so may have some small element of compassion within them.

Emilié listened to what the boss said to her (in English), but of course could not understand the conversations between the gang members. That said, by 'listening with her eyes' and observing the behaviour and body language of the insurgents, Emilié was able to discern that they seemed to engage in a high level of disagreement amongst themselves. She surmised that this uncertainty and internal disagreement might work in her favour.

Emilié had lots of time to think.

As day one merged into day two, that became day three, and in turn day four, Emilié's contact with the boss increased. By listening, trying to understand the motives of the rebels and persuading them that she was of no value to them, she convinced the boss that, whilst the authorities would no doubt be looking for her now, she was probably going to be more of a liability to them than a prized asset. After all, they had wanted to capture an American for political reasons, and so what value can a young girl from an extremely small and relatively unimportant country be to them?

But Emilié did something else. She said she had asthma and needed her medicine and inhaler, which of course she no longer had. She said that her medical condition was controlled when she had her medicine, but when without it the asthma intensified. Emilié had cleverly acted as if she were having increased breathing and hyperventilating difficulties over the previous hours. She got the idea when she reflected on the fact that on day one she was genuinely hyperventilating out of sheer fear. Her strategy was to keep this up, artificially, and to increase the frequency and intensity of her hyperventilation.

Emilié explained that if she couldn't get her medicine, then she would become progressively ill and a liability to them. She appealed to the human side of the leader to release her. This, combined with the fact that she was not the prized asset they thought they'd captured, was sufficient for him to show leniency. Emilié was released on the fifth day.

HOW CAN I USE THIS?

Emilié's eight key lessons are transferrable to more 'normal' aspects of life and negotiations:

1. Find the ultimate decision-maker; don't waste time with those who do not have the power or authority to negotiate.
2. Even though it might pain you to do so, make the higher authority figure feel important; appeal to and stroke their ego.
3. Remain composed when others are trying to put you under pressure; hold your nerve. If you lose control or panic, then you will not be thinking clearly and you're likely to make irrational decisions.
4. Think about the situation from the other party's perspective – what do they have to gain or lose, and how does this inform what you do and what you say?
5. Have patience; let the passing of time work against the other party, if possible.
6. Appeal to the good nature, moral values and sympathies of the other party.

Other than psychopaths, nobody wants to be accused of directly or indirectly harming someone who is vulnerable, defenceless or disadvantaged.

7. Use a 'red herring' (illustrated in case 49 and described further in Part Two), to pretend you want or need something else which is very important (asthma inhaler in this case) in order to get what you really want.

8. When faced with an extreme situation or unacceptable behaviour from the other side then you have every right to use every dirty trick you can think of – including lying and deception.

52 RUSSIAN FRONT

52 RUSSIAN FRONT

Liz, a union leader at Plassano Pressings, was preparing for her usual, annual pay negotiations with the company directors, primarily Frank, the HR Director. She was confident of agreeing the usual annual inflation increase, plus loyalty bonuses for members who have many years' service. After all, for the past few years this is the way things have gone.

Liz: *'Frank, we've laid out our terms, which we hope you will be able to agree with. They're in line with the national inflation rate, plus of course our standard increments for those members with substantial years of continuous service.'*

Frank: *'Yes, Liz, we've received your demands. To avoid wasting your time, or ours, I need to let you know that this year there will be a pay freeze. So, any discussion of pay rises are not on the table, and neither are the previous "generous allowances" accorded for length of service. In fact, you should be grateful we're not tabling a pay reduction, given the state of the economy and the performance of the business – which this year will make a loss.'*

Liz: *'Frank, in all my years here there has never been a pay freeze. Typically, we've managed to agree a pay increase of something between 3–5% for our members, plus the annual service year's increase. A pay freeze is totally unacceptable and if that's all that's on the table, we will be balloting our members for strike action. To quote someone more famous than me, "We will fight you on the beaches"!'*

Frank: *'Liz, we're in the West Midlands of the UK, so why you would want to go more than 100 miles to the beach at a time like this escapes me!'*

Liz: *'Do you think this is funny? These are our union members' livelihoods that we're talking about here.'*

Frank: *'No, it's not funny, so stop using dramatic cliché's like that and, more to the point, I agree with you. Yes, exactly, it's the livelihoods of our employees that you need to be thinking about right now. Threatening a strike when the whole country is in the middle of a financial crisis, when other employers are making people redundant left, right and centre, and when anything that threatens the viability of our company means we will probably need to make significant job cuts is, frankly, irresponsible. Is that the announcement you would like to make to your members – that we need to lose 15% of our employees by Christmas?'*

Within the same meeting Plassano Pressings offered something better, but they held on to, and achieved their primary objective, which was a pay freeze for the coming 12 months.

The offer was a choice between relinquishing some precious terms and conditions, especially 'double-rate overtime', in order to create a pay pot to allow for an increase this year, or to sign up to a three-year pay deal where there is a pay freeze in year one, with a guarantee of a minimum 2% pay increase in both years two and three.

Faced with the choice, the union members made it clear to Liz that their precious terms and conditions were more important than a short-term pay rise. They swiftly signed up to the three-year deal.

SEQUEL

The company achieved their primary objective – a pay freeze.

Twelve months later, no forced redundancies had been made, though natural staff turnover meant the company could reduce its salary bill and Plassano Pressings continues to trade.

In year two, as promised, Plassano implemented a 2% pay rise across the board. They found enough cash to support this… just.

The future is unknown.

All parties remain nervous.

INSIGHTS AND LEARNING

The term 'Russian Front' describes a situation in which one party presents the other with just two options. One option is so awful (like being sent to fight on the cold and frozen Russian Front) that the other party readily and relatively quickly agrees to the alternative, as it is the least worst option.

The Russian Front option may not be completely awful, but it's almost certainly one the other party will not choose. Two options are being presented, but there is only one that's acceptable – in effect, there is only one option.

Another use of Russian Front is as a more overt threat, as in *"If you do not agree to X, then you leave me no option other than to do Y"*. Taking course Y is framed as an inevitable consequence of the other party not agreeing to X. The disadvantages will be explained to make the anticipated pain of consequence Y feel real and vivid. Offering something that is clearly undesirable creates panic and discomfort, something that the other party will want to move away from. In this case, Liz, and her union members, considered a pay freeze as the least worst option.

That said, it wasn't totally one-sided. The union felt that whilst conceding something significant (no pay rise this year), they did 'win' something in return (years two and three at a guaranteed minimum pay increase), plus they got to keep their jobs.

They also felt they had a choice. People like to feel they have a choice in matters that are important to them. The fact that they had little choice is irrelevant. When playing the game of negotiation, there are often subtler factors and influences in play. Even when both parties know exactly what's going on, it does not prevent them from 'playing' the roles required of the game in order to achieve the best result possible.

Even in the face of a 'Russian Front', people like to save face.

HOW CAN I USE THIS?

When you only have one option, how many options do you have?

The 'Russian Front' tactic appears to be offering two options, but, in reality, one of them is so horrible you only have one option.

Or do you even have one?

'One option' may indeed be one option, but, technically, you don't have any option at all – you have no option, because one option is not an 'option'.

Or, do you theoretically still have two options, i.e. you could, for some inexplicable reason, take the more horrible option?

Do you in fact have three options, i.e. take either option one or option two, or decide upon a third option, which is to walk away?

Even better, could you have four options; the fourth being to create a brand-new option yourself and to present that as an alternative? There would have been multiple possibilities in the case above, considering the range of variables involved in such negotiations – it's not just about pay.

Or, do you have five options? Wow, this is getting better! The fifth being to negotiate a better option *with* the other party, on the basis that if you put your heads together, you may jointly be able to create a solution that so far neither of you have thought of?

Technical arguments aside (0–5 or more options), if presented with a 'Russian Front' yourself:

- Don't agree to being confined to just two options, say, *'Yes, those are certainly two possibilities; now let's look at some more.'*

- State that being presented with two options, where one is unacceptable, is actually just one option, and point this out to them as being unreasonable.

- Realise that you have more options; a third being to walk away (not accepting either option) and others, by inventing even more by being creative yourself or by appealing to the other party for you to put your heads together to explore other possibilities.

- Be assertive, call out their behaviour by saying you think they're being too narrow in their thinking, and ask whether they're prepared to work with you to create alternatives – if they refuse, they portray themselves as unreasonable.

- Whenever a nasty tactic is exposed it loses most, if not all, of its power, so let them know you know what they're doing by saying something like, *'Goodness me, next you'll be sending me to the Russian Front!'*

- Finally, you may choose to walk away as a matter of principle, even if it does entail risk or is disadvantageous to you in the short term, because that may prompt them to reconsider and be more reasonable. It's only when one party threatens to, or actually does, walk away that true positions surface – try it occasionally, it can be fun to walk away – with your pride and principles intact. Just don't make a habit of it!

52 REAL-LIFE NEGOTIATION CASES

PART TWO: DEFINITIONS AND EXPLANATION OF TERMS

DEFINITIONS AND EXPLANATION OF TERMS

Some books include either an index and/or a glossary of terms. Typically, these are just one-sentence descriptions of vocabulary.

In this book simple one-sentence descriptors are not likely to be sufficient because, as mentioned in the Introduction, negotiation has its own 'language'. Hence, Part Two of this book describes, in some detail, the more important terms used in the cases in Part One.

Some are specific to the practice, art and science of negotiation, others are more general, but nevertheless have a particular relevance to the subject. All have been referred to in one or more cases within Part One.

In view of the importance of these negotiation terms and concepts, you're encouraged to read this section in full, rather than just using it as a 'terminology look-up tool'. Some small portions of text from Part One are repeated here in order to reinforce key points and enhance learning.

A

ANCHORING

Anchoring is one of the shortcuts that people use in making calculations and estimating numbers, especially when they don't know where to start.

The human mind is heavily influenced by the first number that's associated with any given situation that calls for estimation of a figure. In business, a common example of anchoring occurs in the list price that suppliers provide. If you secure a 10% discount off the list price during a negotiation, do you actually know if this new price is a good or a bad deal? It's 10% off of a number that's not necessarily based on anything real, such as the supplier's costs or the market price.

To overcome this bias you first need to recognise it. So, if a recruiter says the price for hiring a new person is 30% of their salary, do not negotiate a % discount from that number, but rather refuse to continue the discussion unless the supplier removes that number (%) from consideration. You can then establish your own anchor – your own starting point. For example – *'I don't deal in percentages; I prefer to establish a fixed fee. I'm prepared to pay $X for you to provide me with a short list, $Y for a successful hire and $Z when the new recruit passes their six-month probationary period. Are you prepared to proceed on that basis?'*

To set your own anchor you need a strong understanding of costs and the market, but by conditioning the other party from early on in the relationship you can use anchoring in your favour. If you're the one doing the selling, then you could cut straight to the chase and say, *'Before we get too deep into this discussion, I need you to understand that the price of X is $13,500. I am happy to continue our discussion if you're happy to proceed on that understanding.'*

See also 'Preconditioning' elsewhere in this section.

B

BARGAINING

Bargaining is a subset of the broader negotiation landscape. Bargaining is important and it is a professional skill, however, it's closer to a more basic skill commonly witnessed in street markets called 'haggling'. Haggling is unsophisticated but often fun, and it almost always involves just one variable – price.

All said, bargaining is a legitimate professional tool in business; seen in automobile showrooms and in multimillion dollar deals. So if you're going to bargain, pitch your initial offer high (seller) or low (buyer), but keep this demand or position reasonable.

Remember that people expect to have to bargain or haggle, so they can feel disappointed if you don't play the game, or more worryingly, they may think that something's wrong if you give in and accept their offer too quickly.

BASKET DEAL

See 'Loss Leader'.

BATNA: BEST ALTERNATIVE TO A NEGOTIATED AGREEMENT

Having a well-developed and attractive BATNA is a great source of power in any negotiation. You can identify your BATNA in a specific situation by asking yourself the question: *'What will I do if this negotiation is not successful?'*

A key reason for entering into a negotiation is to achieve a better outcome than would be possible without negotiating. Paradoxically, one of the greatest dangers in a negotiation is being too committed to reaching agreement without sufficient consideration of alternatives. You get so wrapped up in the details of the deal that you fail to take a broader perspective. As a consequence, you may fail to get the best deal you could have achieved.

So, having a clearly thought out BATNA, or a range of alternative courses of action open to you (including the power to walk away from an unsatisfactory negotiation), gives you considerable power. You don't actually have to walk away or pursue another course of action, it's the fact that you have other options that gives you the confidence to negotiate from a stronger position. Also, if the other party knows (or believes) you have alternatives, this can further tip the balance of power in your direction.

BLUFF

Let's be honest, if you bluff you're lying.

Using bluff is a legitimate negotiation tactic, though you need to be very brave, extremely confident, or at least be able to fake the confidence that comes from a powerful position. You also need to be prepared in case it backfires. Bluffing is, of course, a dangerous game, as the other person may call your bluff.

Equally, if you're going to call someone's bluff, for example by saying, *'Okay, but if you do X, then I have no alternative than to respond with Y'*, then you had better be prepared to follow through with 'Y'.

Bluff can work when the other party believes what is said and feels they must act or concede in order to avoid a problem. It can also work if the other party thinks they're going to lose something they already have, lose an opportunity to gain something, or they simply want to maintain the status quo.

Tread with care, and if you're going to use bluff perhaps you should reserve it for times when you have few other, more professional negotiation tools and tactics available.

BOTTLENECK

When you consider that a bottleneck literally refers to the top narrow part of a bottle, it becomes clear that in business operations it refers to a phenomenon where the performance or capacity of an entire system is limited by a single or small number of components or resources.

If you're buying a product or service that's in short supply, even if of relatively low value, then if you cannot get it in time (or sufficient numbers of a product, volume of a raw material, or you cannot guarantee continuity of supply over time), then your whole operation can be in jeopardy.

If you've pre-paid for a long-haul holiday or important business trip and you cannot get your travel visa in time, then this is a low-cost (the price of the visa), but high negative consequence bottleneck, which may result in massive financial loss and cancellation of your plans for the next couple of weeks – with further negative consequences.

Of course it depends on the situation, but bottlenecks can generally be avoided or dealt with by allowing plenty of buffer time before you actually need the product or service, by holding sufficient buffer stock, by exploring alternatives that bypass the bottleneck, or by re-engineering the end product or service that the component is part of.

BRINKMANSHIP

Brinkmanship means going right to the edge in terms of either pushing an issue as far as possible or in refusing to agree a deal as a seemingly fixed deadline approaches. At the time of writing, the Greek financial crisis is still playing out. We have witnessed several standoffs between the Greek government and institutions such as the European Central Bank, as deadline after repayment deadline approach, and then at the last minute another bailout rescues the situation or the Greek government accede to another demand that they previously rejected outright. These are clear examples of brinkmanship.

Brinkmanship relies a great deal on bluff and on who can hold out the longest. The hope from the party playing this tactic is that the other side will give in first. It's a risky game and it requires a great deal of skill and nerve to avoid falling over the brink, resulting in a lose-lose outcome. Bluffing is a risky game and if you're going to bluff, you need to know what you will do if your bluff is called, (see 'Bluff' earlier in this section.)

When faced with a brinkmanship stance/demand you should hold your nerve; do not allow yourself to become rattled; remain cool and calm. Yes, it's easier said than done, but nobody ever said that negotiations are easy!

If the nature of the tactic is an imposed deadline, try to signal that you have plenty of time and that, if needed, you can negotiate more time for yourself internally/ externally (which may or may not be the case).

If the other party asks for a decision today, say something like, *'Okay, if you want my decision today, then I will give it to you. My decision is "no". If you want a different decision, then you need to give me more time.'*

However, be careful in counter-bluffing; it may result in a lose-lose standoff, or you may end up being the overall loser. If it is the other party's imposed deadline, then simply point out to them that *their* deadline is approaching; it's not your deadline; you did not impose it, they did.

You could suggest that to prevent them from rushing too hastily into an ill thought out deal, they renegotiate the timescale themselves, or buy more time from their side.

Alternatively, indicate that if the deadline is really non-negotiable then, sadly, on this occasion, it would appear that it won't be possible to achieve a negotiated agreement within their time frame. You appreciate that they're under time pressure, but that's not your problem.

BROKEN RECORD

Like an old vinyl record that's stuck in the same groove, the Broken Record tactic involves repeating over and over again the point or demand you're making.

This will sometimes work because the other party gets fed up with the constant repetition, and they may feel that progress is unlikely until this obstacle is removed. Broken record emphasises the need for persistence in negotiation and a refusal to accept 'No' at its face value without testing or pushback.

Examples include, *'I'm sorry, but you will have to do better than that', 'I may have mentioned that price is the most important thing here'*, and *'As I have said more than four times now, unless you can guarantee delivery within seven days of confirmation of order, we will need to place the business elsewhere.'*

It's not the most elegant of tactics, and in some ways it's crude, stubborn or even childish in nature. However, if you're faced with it, what can you do?

Say that you've clearly heard the request, however, without any possibility of flexibility or negotiation on this point from their side it's difficult to see how a negotiated agreement will be possible. State that making demands is not a 'negotiation' as you understand it, it's an ultimatum, and you do not negotiate when put into such a constraining and inflexible position.

Alternatively, play your own broken record, as in *'I understand your standard payment terms are 90 days from end of month of invoice; you've made that very clear. However, that's totally unacceptable for us as a supplier. I repeat that I do not believe our request for payment within 60 days of submission of invoice is unreasonable, especially as you will have had the goods for two full months.'*

Tell them that, whilst you hear them on this issue, it's possible that if you can 'park' it for a while and talk about other variables, you may be able to find a solution that means everyone is happy.

BUYING SIGNAL

A buying signal is simply that – a signal from one party to another, often sent unconsciously and unintentionally, that the other person is interested or indeed ready to buy.

The signals can be verbal, as in inquiring about the price of an item, asking questions about details, exploring how they could use a product or how a service might work in practice, etc. However, they could also be non-verbal such as picking up a product, spending some time examining it, putting it in their shopping basket (pretty self-explanatory), or a more subtle change in body state such as relaxing, using different gestures or looking inside their wallet.

When people avoid eye contact with you, say that they're *'just looking'*, are briefly glancing at a wide range of products, or simply meandering or moving around a showroom quickly, then these are unlikely to be people who are about to get their cash out!

C

CALLING THE BEHAVIOUR

When someone is acting in a way that's not helpful to the negotiation process, then you can metaphorically 'step out' of the detail of the negotiation itself – the content – and talk about what you see and hear happening in terms of behaviour and process.

This is called 'calling the behaviour'; effectively pointing out to the other party that what you see them doing is not helpful to either of you, and to appeal to them to change tack.

Reasonable people will respond positively to this. Unreasonable ones will not, or will become annoyed that you've discovered their tactic(s). In the latter case, you need to ask yourself if this is a person who you want to continue to negotiate with, or whether your time would be spent more fruitfully pursuing other options.

CARTEL

A cartel is a distorted market situation in which similar suppliers cooperate with each other. Their intention is to preserve and grow their profitability by maintaining prices at a high level and by restricting competition.

Even if anti-competitive behaviour is illegal in some jurisdictions, it does not mean that cartels do not exist.

See also 'Monopolist' elsewhere in this section for some ideas on how to deal with monopolistic or limited competition situations.

CLIMATE/ATMOSPHERE

There are many things that you can influence, or even control, that will determine the negotiation climate.

Before you do anything, however, you need to ask yourself, 'What sort of climate do I want to create?'

You may want an open, friendly, collaborative, supportive climate, particularly if you're negotiating with long-term partners or you want to encourage the other party to open up and to work with you on problem solving. Alternatively, you may have a serious issue to resolve. The other party might have made a mistake or let you down repeatedly, so a more formal, direct, 'down-to-business' or even austere climate may be more in line with your objectives. You can be firm without being nasty to create the right climate to support your goals.

Things to consider that can influence the climate include the venue, dress code, room layout, seating and table arrangements, distance between the various parties, room temperature and ventilation, refreshments, the agenda, greetings, whether there's an office or factory tour to see facilities or to meet other people informally, degree of rapport, empathy and the speed with which the negotiation proceeds, etc. Yes, that was a deliberately long sentence, in order to demonstrate just how many things there are to consider that contribute towards the negotiation climate or atmosphere.

COGNITIVE DISSONANCE

Cognitive dissonance is the mental discomfort experienced by a person who holds two or more contradictory thoughts at the same time, or is confronted by new information that conflicts with existing beliefs, ideas or values.

In negotiation this is most often found when a person finds out, after an agreement has been concluded, that they could have secured a better deal elsewhere, or even an improved deal with that same party.

It happens when things change significantly, new information comes to light or, even worse, when you only latterly discover information that was plain to see all along, if only you had taken the time to find it.

Firstly, the best way to avoid this is to do your research and due diligence to uncover the relevant facts and benchmarks before you go into a negotiation. Knowledge is power. Again, easy to say, but equally easy to overlook or skip, especially when you are busy.

Secondly, be clear about your target(s), your limits and what would constitute a good deal, (see 'LIM', later in this section).

Finally, if you later discover that you did not achieve the best deal, then don't beat yourself up unnecessarily about it afterwards. Tomorrow is another day; just ensure you benefit from the situation by learning for next time.

COMMODITY

A commodity is a raw material or primary agricultural product that can be bought and sold, such as copper, oil, wheat or coffee. Commodities are often used as inputs to the production of other higher value goods or services.

The idea of a commodity is that it is interchangeable with other supplies of the same type. The quality of a given commodity may differ slightly, for example different grades of coffee bean, but for some it's essentially the same thing; a barrel of oil is a barrel of oil, regardless of where you buy it.

Technological advances have also led to new types of commodities being exchanged in the marketplace: for example, cell phone minutes and bandwidth; you can't put those in a sack or barrel, but they can be bought and sold.

COMMON ENEMY

Identifying or creating a common enemy is about one party trying to get the other to see that they're not fighting each other, but rather they're together fighting some other third party – a shared adversary.

This can create a strengthening sense of *'it's you and me together'*, and it can promote a greater spirit of collaboration between two parties who initially might have been negotiating against each other.

An example would be a supplier who has a great relationship with a manufacturing manager in a factory. He tries to imply that the 'common enemy' is the factory's head of purchasing, who's trying to prevent the manufacturing manager from getting the latest piece of equipment that the supplier provides, and which the manufacturing manager desperately wants.

COMPROMISING

The five main negotiation styles are to compete, accommodate, avoid, collaborate or compromise. The first four are more 'noticeable' as they're extremes. Compromise, however, seems to be somewhere in the middle.

Whilst most professional business negotiations aim for collaboration, it's rare to achieve a pure 'win-win' situation in which the deal is 100% optimised for all parties. For one-off transactional negotiations a more competing style may be quicker and give you the best outcome. Damage limitation may involve an accommodating style from one party, and avoidance and can also be strategically applied in some situations – perhaps when you need time to think or gather information, or you're not ready to negotiate just yet.

So, if we can't always achieve the perfect win-win, or a collaborative style is not appropriate, the next best thing may be to aim for a mutually agreed compromise.

To some people, a compromise is a realistic end-point resulting from two strong negotiating parties, each with initially conflicting starting positions, who thrash out the best deal they can between them, and who both walk away happy with the end result.

Some others view a compromise as a sort of sub-optimal 'win-win', or even a situation in which both parties come away with half a lose! Is your glass half full or half empty?

One thing's for sure, any negotiation must involve some element of compromise – otherwise it's not a negotiation.

However, because most negotiations involve multiple variables it's possible for one party to accept less of X, whilst the other takes more of X but gives in on some or all of Y. So, the best compromises do not revolve around just one variable, such as haggling over price. With multiple variables, and intelligent compromise, it's possible for both parties to walk away more than 50% happy. That's good, its not a full win-win outcome, but both parties are happy to have what they have, and its what we call 'good business'.

Compromise is an appropriate style to use when an issue is not worth the effort to be negotiated in full, a temporary settlement to a complex matter is needed or an expedient solution under time pressure is required. It's also appropriate when both parties are adopting a competitive stance, and consequently little progress is being made, or when the negotiation is in its closing stages and a relatively small compromise by both parties on one or more variables will seal the deal.

CONCESSIONS

A concession is something that one party gives to the other. However, best negotiation practice states that you should not give something away without receiving something in return. Thus, you should 'trade' concessions; you give something to another party that they value, but which is relatively easy for you to give, in return for them providing you with something else, something different, that you value, but which does not cost them a great deal.

If you simply give something away in the hope that the other party will reciprocate in some undefined or guaranteed way, i.e. without agreeing something specific in return, then you've not only weakened your position, you've also opened yourself to exploitation as the receiver may expect you to give away other things unconditionally.

Note that the principle of 'reciprocity' (see later in this section) is powerful in building relationships. This can even be helpful when, as pointed out above, what you give away has little value to you or costs you nothing; for example, buying the other party a coffee or emailing them a useful article. However, in business negotiations, where concessions can have significant value, you should only offer a concession conditional on you receiving something tangible in return. It's not just good business sense... it's common sense.

So, from your perspective, and in a specific situation, consider what you can offer to the other party that has relatively higher value to them than it does to you, and what they can offer, which may not cost them much, but which helps you to meet your objectives.

Finally, trading concessions is also helpful in speeding up negotiations, as with each trade both parties move further towards agreement. It creates a sense of progression and narrows the range of those things that are yet to be agreed.

COST DRIVERS

Cost drivers are the key elements that contribute towards or influence the cost of a product or service.

In a factory there is the cost of running the machinery in terms of labour hours, electricity, floor space, etc. A cost driver of 'maintenance', for example, would be the number of hours a machine is run before it needs to be maintained.

Activity Based Costing is based on the belief that activities cause costs and, therefore, a link should be established between those activities and the end product or service. The cost drivers, thus, are the link between the activities and the cost. For a product it could be as simple as labour hours and for a service it could be the same, as in the time taken to manage a project.

In sales and marketing, typical cost drivers are the number of salespeople required, or the number of advertisements that need to be placed to achieve a certain sales revenue.

All businesses have costs, and some are not so obvious. What about the costs of returned goods, re-work or the number of service calls required to fix a problem? In manufacturing, what about the cost of not running the machinery or having staff standing idle if a key component part is not available? See also, 'Bottleneck' in this section.

COUNTER-OFFER

This is an offer made in response to a proposal made by the other party that you consider to be unacceptable in some way. Their proposal may be attractive, or moving in the right direction, but it's not yet at a point you're prepared to accept.

Making a counter-offer shows that you're clear about your goals and you're not going to simply say 'yes' to the first offer. It also allows negotiations to continue, perhaps more on your terms than the other party's.

When someone makes an offer, and it's then accepted, it's difficult for the person making the offer to then withdraw it. However, when a counter-offer is made it effectively voids/rejects the first party's offer, and so the second party cannot later insist that the original offer be honoured.

One way of making offers that are less 'binding' is to use hypothetical language, such as, *'How would you feel about X?'* or *'What would you say if I were to propose Y?'*

See also 'Hypothesising' elsewhere in this section.

D

DEADLINES

A deadline is a date or time by which a certain action needs to be taken. Historically, it derives from a line around a prison beyond which prisoners could be shot dead.

Deadlines are an important sub-dimension of time. Deadlines can be imposed by one party or, and this is significant, they can be agreed by both. They can encourage both parties to concentrate on creative solutions and/or create urgency for concessions.

However, beware this does not lead to reckless solutions, or cause you to give in too early, for fear of losing a deal.

As stating false deadlines are a common tactic you shouldn't over-react. Simply make a note of the deadline indicated, avoid further discussion about it, and become a little brisker in your approach. Remember, it's their deadline not yours, so when the deadline gets nearer remind them that their deadline is approaching, and that if they're to meet it they'll need to flex their position and/or proposition.

You can of course impose real or imaginary deadlines yourself in order to accelerate the negotiation process or achieve an earlier closure. Just be careful if you're bluffing, and be prepared for the consequences, (see 'Bluff' elsewhere in this section.)

DEADLOCK

A deadlock is a position in a negotiation where it appears no progress can be made due to fundamental differences or disagreements.

Deadlock can arise when parties become entrenched in their own, divergent positions, one party's demands are seen by the other as being unreasonable, personal egos get in the way, or when multiple parties with divergent goals are involved.

Actions to break deadlock can include: changing from a 'competitive' to a 'cooperative' approach; treating the deadlock as a joint problem that needs to be jointly solved; finding a concession that's easy or not expensive for you to make but valuable to the receiver; and asking the other party for a concession that's cheap for them but more valuable to you. You can also propose a combination of concessions from both sides.

Additionally, you can suggest a break, perhaps to allow emotions to cool, use humour, or simply point out that both sides seem to be losing perspective and heading for a 'lose-lose' outcome.

You may decide to change one or more members of the team in order to shift the 'personality dynamic', break down the problem in order to deal with, and agree smaller issues one by one, to get some genuine movement and to build a sense of agreement.

You could also introduce a deadline, either real or artificial, to create a sense of urgency and a 'make or break' moment, introduce new information or place a different emphasis or perspective on existing issues.

See also 'Hypothesising' and 'Deadlines' elsewhere in this section.

DESPERATION

In negotiations you should never appear desperate. Even if you are, as soon as the other party senses you need to close the deal urgently they may use pressure of time to force you to concede more, and sooner.

Showing desperation diminishes your power – massively! So, disguise any sense of urgency; never say 'yes' to the first offer or 'yes' too quickly. Intimate that you have time, plenty of it, and that you have other options. Be careful not to 'leak' any sense of urgency through your body language, what you say or the way in which you say it.

DIRECT PROCUREMENT VS. INDIRECT PROCUREMENT

Direct procurement is the act of acquiring raw materials and goods for production. These purchases are generally done in large quantities, acquired from a pool of suppliers at the best possible cost, quality and reliability. These purchases are made frequently and are necessary for key business operations. If key raw materials become unavailable, then they can cause a 'bottleneck' (see elsewhere in this section).

Indirect procurement is the act of purchasing products and services to keep a business going. They do not necessarily add to a business's bottom line, and sometimes those who do not take a holistic view of the way in which a business operates disparagingly refer them to as 'costs' to the business rather than generators of revenue. Indirect procurement can add revenue-generating value however, such as training the sales force to be more effective, to close more sales and at more profitable rates.

Indirect procurement includes things such as maintenance, buying office supplies, software, catering, recruitment, training and consultancy. Without indirect procurement functions, businesses wouldn't be able to operate effectively.

DISTRIBUTIVE BARGAINING

See 'Zero-Sum Game'.

DUE DILIGENCE

See 'Negotiation Criteria'.

E

ELEPHANT IN THE ROOM

The expression 'the elephant in the room' refers to the obvious issue that is either being ignored or that nobody wants to address. It's sometimes referred to as the 'moose in the corner'; everyone knows it's there, everyone can see it, everyone can smell it but nobody wants to mention it!

Often, the longer the elephant or moose is ignored the bigger and 'smellier' it gets.

Dealing with such issues requires courage, but the payoff can be significant, and often a relief to all concerned that someone has finally put it on the table and tackled it. Note, you would probably need quite a strong table!

When the parties are not talking about the real issue in a negotiation, then little progress is likely to be made.

Identify it, get it out, name it, deal with it and move on and, please… someone go and get a bucket and mop!

EMOTION

There's a big difference between using emotion and getting emotional.

The former is a conscious, intelligent application of a legitimate influencing strategy designed to produce a desired outcome. The latter, when it's a negative emotion, is pathetic, weak, irrational, foolish, crazy, disturbing, egotistical, sad, etc.

The key thing to remember is that when a person allows themself to get emotional they lose a very important thing… they lose control.

Negotiators who get emotional stop listening; they become unpredictable, lose focus and make poor decisions. Consequently, they often hurt themselves and don't meet their goals.

By losing self-control they forfeit control over the situation and the other party. They may say things they later regret, dig their heels into a position they cannot easily get out of, or reject good deals out of spite. More damagingly, the focus can shift from working out a good solution to one of trying to hurt the other party.

In negotiations you can express an emotion without demonstrating it, i.e. you can tell the other party that you're feeling frustrated by the lack of progress within a negotiation without exhibiting frustration in front of them. You tell them how you are feeling without physically spluttering, spurting, stammering, stamping and shouting.

You can also act out an emotion. You can pretend to get emotional in order to unsettle the other party, destabilise the situation or to try to extract a concession. However, whilst this may work occasionally, if you regularly raise your voice, bang the table or walk out of negotiations then this blunt tactic loses its power. You will also lose respect, credibility and destroy relationships along the way.

Emotion is powerful; a wise person uses it wisely and unemotionally.

ESCALATION

In the context of negotiation this can mean several things. It can mean that demands are escalated, for example a price increase is asked for or a demand is made in relation to some other variable. This is escalation of a specific demand i.e. making the requirement more demanding.

Alternatively, escalation can mean that an important decision, such as the agreement to a deal be escalated to a higher level of decision-making authority, perhaps because the other party is unable, or unwilling to agree to what is being asked for.

Escalation of demands can be countered by calling the other party's bluff, by making a counter proposal of your own, by changing the configuration of the deal, by asking for a recess, or by threatening to or actually walking away from the table.

Escalation of decision making is common, particularly when deals are nearing conclusion, or they become larger or more complex. In such cases it's common for the decision makers who are 'above' both negotiating parties to get involved to seal the deal. Curiously, this can even happen when the parties at the table have the mandate to agree. Sometimes one or other feels the need to check back with their boss, or more dis-empowering, their boss decides to check-in with them before the deal is finalised.

See also 'Higher Authority' elsewhere in this section.

EXPLOITABLE

See 'Nuisance'.

F

FATALISM VS. DETERMINISM

Fatalism is a belief that events are determined by fate.

People who subscribe to fatalism believe they have to accept the outcome of events and they cannot do anything to change the outcome. This is because events are determined by something over which they have no control – a higher power, for example. Cultures that tend to adopt a more fatalistic view of the world include those from the Middle East, India and Pakistan.

Fatalism can portray itself in business and negotiations by apparent apathy, a stated inability to significantly influence events, delaying proceedings, sidestepping issues, avoiding confrontation or tackling conflicting views head on. In the Middle East there is a strong belief in 'Insha'Allah', which means 'God willing' or 'if Allah wills'.

In contrast, the North American culture tends to believe that it is possible to control, or at least influence events. Failing this, even in the irrefutable reality that outcomes and results cannot be changed, there still appears to exist the freedom to choose how to respond without being compelled to react in a certain way by forces beyond their control.

North Americans tend towards a 'determinism' outlook as in *we can influence this, we can control this, we can do this*', most aptly portrayed by president Obama's phrase, 'Yes, we can!'

FLINCH

A Flinch is any physical and/or verbal response that indicates that you're surprised (usually adversely) at what you've just heard or been shown.

It does not have to be the physical recoil of your whole body, an astonished look, a scream or uttered obscenity. In fact, it's best in professional circles to keep such reactions under control. If this proves difficult, then prescribed medication may be an option, and you can buy a special white jacket with long arms that you can ask a willing colleague to tie behind your back!

Being more serious... even subtle flinching, such as raising your eyebrows, or a short intake of breath when presented with a proposal or request from the other party, is a good way of signalling that what they've just suggested is extraordinary or in some way unacceptable.

If flinching is not your style, or is not appropriate for cultural reasons, then look dumbstruck and say nothing. This puts the onus on the other party to explain what they have just said or requested; weakening their case and giving you time to think.

The skilled 'flincher' is hoping that the other party will immediately improve their offer or 'qualify' it as in… *'Of course that's the price including delivery and tax',* or… *'But I'm sure we can improve on that offer for you.'* Inexperienced negotiators fall for the flinch trap and often end up leaving money on the table, that they rightfully should have had.

So what do you do when someone flinches at you? How do you avoid leaving money on the table?

- Stay silent, remain calm and composed, do not show any meaningful response; say nothing and wait for them to respond verbally.

- If they still say nothing, restate your case and ask for their response to your proposal.

- Recognise that they're probably doing it deliberately and 'smile internally' to yourself, as you know it's not going to work on you – refuse to be ruffled.

- If they then make a counter-proposal, use the same tactic - flinch in whatever way seems appropriate, without turning the negotiation into a circus act!

- Politely suggest that perhaps this deal is not within their price range, and you're more than happy to propose an alternative that better suits their budget.

FUNNY MONEY

When quoting prices or asking for concessions it is common for sellers to try to make what they're asking for seem small or trivial, for example, *'We're only talking about 2% more than you were expecting to pay', 'It's only $2 per unit price increase on a $147 item'* or *'It only amounts to €50 per day'*. Sellers will talk about monthly, weekly or daily costs, whereas what they're really proposing is an annual fee of many multiples of that, which they want to take as an up-front payment. Alternatively, they may talk about low initial payments, when in fact the ramp-up in future years becomes prohibitive.

Buyers will try to diminish the size of the discount they're requesting by saying it is only 3%, when in fact the capital equipment costs millions of dollars, so they're really talking about a huge discount in absolute terms off the quotation.

What each person is trying to do is to diminish the absolute amount (often cost) of what they're asking for, so as to make it, and perhaps the other party, seem petty – and in many cases we're not talking about 'petty' cash.

When faced with the 'funny money' tactic simply translate the amount or percentage into a form that serves your position, and point this out to the other party.

G

GOOD COP BAD COP

Famously demonstrated in US cop shows, 'good cop, bad cop', or 'good guy, bad guy' is one of the oldest, best-known and most quoted negotiation tactics.

In a meeting with two or more people from the other side, one person behaves in a difficult manner, asking challenging and confrontational questions, making extreme demands and appearing less interested in negotiating a mutually agreeable solution. They may even become aggressive and make threats. Their role is to create an uncomfortable tension and to put pressure on you.

Then another person steps in and takes a more pleasant and agreeable approach. The 'good cop' may even apologise for the 'bad cop's' behaviour, but they appeal to the other party to be reasonable and to comply because if they don't, then the bad cop may make things very unpleasant. Whereas the bad cop causes tension, the good cop creates a source of escape and resolution, or the promise of avoidance of pain.

If you encounter this approach, expose both of them for what they're doing and let them know that it's not going to work on you. Remind yourself that they're both on the same side, and so negotiate with them on that basis. Don't let the supposedly nice behaviour of one of them unduly influence you – be tough and resilient with both. Use their behaviour to undermine them, as in *'Look guys, it seems the two of you are not fully aligned in terms of approach or what you want. Why don't we take a break to give you chance to discuss amongst yourselves and then we can resume the negotiation?'*

GUILT

Trying to make the other party feel guilty is a tactic designed to appeal to the good nature, moral values and sympathies of another person.

It's difficult to argue with a moral appeal, especially if the request is to help a person or people from a vulnerable or disadvantaged group. If you believe the plea to be genuine, then maybe you simply do what you can to help.

However, if you suspect a more sinister motive, you should keep a cool head and stay focused on the rational business case.

Guilt could also be used to appeal to you to reciprocate in some way to another person who's done you a favour in the past. Again, this may be entirely legitimate and fair, in which case maybe a return favour is the right thing for you to do. However, if you do not believe it to be justified, or you did not ask for the previous favour in the first place, (it was given to you in the way that free chocolates are presented to you on a plate at the end of a meal, along with a restaurant bill signed with a smiley face!), then you can take a harder line.

You can refer back to the contract, keeping everything objective and above board. Be hard on the issues but respectful of the people.

H

HAGGLING

Haggling is an unsophisticated, yet can also be a fun part of trading, commonly witnessed in street markets in warm climates.

Haggling almost always involves just one variable – price. He wants 20, you offer 10; he comes down to 16 and you up your offer to 14. In the end you agree to split the difference at 15. You walk away thinking you negotiated well, getting him to drop his price from 20 to 15, meanwhile he pockets your cash knowing he would have been happy to sell for 8 and still make a decent profit!

See also 'Bargaining' and 'Cognitive Dissonance', elsewhere in this section

'HELP ME TO HELP YOU'

This expression is a powerful appeal to the other party to be reasonable and/or to behave in a way that enables both parties to move forward in a positive way.

It can most usefully be employed when the other party is being difficult, withholding information or not being particularly cooperative.

The power of the phrase lies in the fact that the appeal is very much in the interests of the person to whom the expression is voiced, i.e. *'If you give me information on this, then you're helping yourself because you're helping me to assist you in achieving what you want.'*

HIGHER AUTHORITY

Referring to a 'higher authority' means you're unable to agree to a concession, or make a final decision because you need approval from someone more senior in your organisation.

The advantages are you can excuse yourself from making a concession or agreeing to something right now; it buys you time to think and it puts indirect pressure on the other party as they may feel the deal is slipping away. They may feel the pressure of delay, or that they now need to do even more to satisfy a more senior, and potentially more demanding decision-maker.

Disadvantages are that it can undermine your own position, both now and in future negotiations, and you may then be bypassed in later discussions. If you use higher authority as a tactic, not entirely truthfully, then be prepared to take the consequences of your deliberate deception.

Of course, as a negotiation progresses the variables and demands may shift beyond your remit, and you then have no choice but to admit that you genuinely need to check in with other people before making a commitment.

Prevention is far better than having to deal with this when it happens, so always establish the authority level of the person(s) you're negotiating with before you get into serious discussions. If you have not, and you now face higher authority, then politely ask that those who are in a position to make a decision be involved in the negotiation. You can also use the tactic yourself and say that as this is now escalating you will need to bring in more senior people from your organisation to conclude the deal.

See also 'Escalation' elsewhere in this section.

HYPOTHESISING

Hypothesising is a helpful technique to 'test the water', to see how serious the other party is. For example, *'If I were to offer you X, how would you feel about doing Y?'*

It's crucial to note that by hypothesising you're not making a firm offer; you're using a question to discover the other party's degree of flexibility and openness, and what it might be possible to agree upon.

Hypothesising can be particularly useful for tabling a new idea, for making suggestions without locking yourself into a firm commitment, for testing out the other party's reaction to an idea, possible solution to a problem, structure of a deal or to help break a deadlock, (see 'Deadlock' elsewhere in this section).

Hypothesising is a very good technique to use in negotiations if you find yourselves dancing around an issue and if neither party has been prepared so far to state a position, request, proposal or demand. It commits you to nothing whilst, at the same time, offering a way forward.

I

IMPACT VS. INTENTION

Sometimes, things get lost in translation. Your intention, the thing you were trying to communicate or achieve, is somehow misinterpreted or has an unintended (usually negative) impact.

It's not always your fault. People tend to hear what they want to hear or they perceive or interpret words and behaviours through their own psychological filters, leading to misunderstanding and further negative consequences.

However, the communicator should take most of the responsibility for transmission of an accurate message. So, make an effort to understand the position of the other party and how they see the situation. Listen actively with an open mind and a desire to create mutual understanding. Apologise if there's been a breakdown in communication, even if you think the fault lies with the other party for not listening or understanding. Say something like… *'I'm sorry, that's not what I meant to say – let me try to say it in a different way.'* Then check for understanding and no bridges have been broken in the process.

If it happens the other way around, you need to give the other party the opportunity to save face by stating that you're certain they did not intend to create the impression that they have, yet that is how they came across to you and/or to others. Give them an opportunity to correct their position or statements so you can jointly move on in the negotiation.

See also 'Saving Face' elsewhere in this section.

IMPLICIT VS. EXPLICIT COMMUNICATION

Implicit communication focuses on the ambiguous areas of gestures, vocal tones, actions and what is not said rather than what is. Implicit communication can be hard to interpret, or can even be misinterpreted, as the recipient can be left confused about the intended message.

Explicit communication, on the other hand, deals with what a person writes or says directly. It can be very clear, direct and straightforward such as, *'No, I am sorry, but I'm not going to do that.'* A person who favoured implicit communication may instead say, *'That would be difficult', 'Maybe'* or *'I'll try.'*

Implicit communication occurs more often in what are referred to as 'high-context cultures', in which people leave many things unsaid. The context, made up of the environment, the situation, and the parties involved, carries messages that match the spoken word and make up for the things that are left unsaid. Indian culture is a high-context culture, as are the cultures of many Asian and Arab nations.

In low-context cultures, such as the US and much of northern Europe, communication is more explicit and so things are often spelled out more clearly and directly. To negotiators from high-context cultures, overt statements might be perceived to be blunt, and questions too penetrating and direct.

There is much room for misunderstanding and frustration within negotiations and business in general if attention is not paid to this very important cultural sub-dimension.[*]

INERTIA

See 'Switching Costs'.

INTERESTS VS. POSITIONS

An 'interest' a person has in something is not necessarily the same as the 'position' they openly take or state.

In case 4 – 'Interests vs. Positions', the following example was given, and is briefly repeated here.

Two office co-workers are arguing about whether or not to have the window open. One opens the window (takes a position), the other gets up and closes it (takes a contrary position). An argument ensues and it appears that a 'win-lose' situation is developing.

However, if each party took time to understand the interest(s) of the other (one wanted fresh air, whilst the other didn't want to sit in a draught), then they could work to find a third solution, a potential 'win-win', such as opening a window at the other end of the room, so that fresh air could enter, but not cause a draught where they're sitting.

---

[*] In several cases within this book, and in some definitions in Part Two, the importance and impact of culture on negotiations has been illustrated and discussed. If you are interested in exploring this aspect further then please contact the author.

Better solutions arise when negotiating parties jointly explore what each person needs and they think creatively to find a resolution that meets both their individual needs and shared interests.

How you approach a negotiation will play a key role in how the negotiation proceeds. Start with an 'I win only if you lose' mentality and you're going to be in for a tough battle and a solution, if any, that's sub-optimal; you will 'leave money on the table'.

If the two colleagues had opened the window halfway, then there would not be enough fresh air for one and still a lesser draught blowing down the neck of the other; both would probably still be dissatisfied and irritated with their respective colleague.

So, in order to find a mutually satisfactory resolution, use questioning and listening, probing and exchanging information, to understand the other party's interests (needs) that lie behind the positions that they take, and constantly reinforce your interest(s) to them.

As mentioned elsewhere in this book, you can also look for low-cost concessions that might have high value to the other person and vice versa. Get creative; the solutions are there if you take time to jointly explore.

Who knows, maybe you've been in this situation and your colleague wants the window open, but you didn't realise it was so they can jump out because they can't stand working with you any longer!

You would never know unless you took the time to understand.

Or maybe you'd prefer it just fine if they saved you both a lot of hassle and jumped?!

J

JOKER

This is when the other party suggests that the proposals you're making are ridiculous and cannot be taken seriously, by using phrases such as, *'You've got to be joking'* or *'Pull the other one.'* The implication is that if you're serious, then there's no prospect of any deal whatsoever.

It's a tactic that could be put in the category of 'bullying'. It's not nice, not particularly professional, but common. The way to deal with this is to remain calm; to not be phased by the sniggers, sneers or snorts from the other side of the table, rephrase your comment and ask that both parties discuss what is possible.

Of course, if your proposal is ridiculous, then you only have yourself to blame for not doing your homework, not understanding the position of the other party or by trying your luck with an outrageous demand.

See also 'Flinch' elsewhere in this section.

L

LAYING DOWN THE GAUNTLET

In the Middle Ages, a gauntlet was the metal glove in a suit of armour, and so by throwing down his defensive gauntlet one knight was challenging another to combat.

In negotiation terms, this does not mean a dual to the death but now rather the presentation of a challenge for another party to meet. The counterparty is given an opportunity to take up the gauntlet, to acknowledge and accept the challenge.

For example, a buyer may say, *'If you meet this price, the deal is yours.'*

A seller may say, *'You've pushed me to my limits. €5,000 is my last offer, pay me that in cash now, and the horse is yours.'*

LAYING DOWN A MARKER

A 'marker' is a stated position, usually numerical, such as price or volume.

When you lay down a marker you put a line in the sand, a starting point, a request, a demand or an offer; for example, a seller may say, 'We *charge £900 for installation*', a buyer may say 'We *can't pay more than €125 per item.*'

Try not to be the first person to lay down a marker. Try to get the other party to state their position first. This gives you information about the 'L' of their LIM Strategy (see 'LIM' elsewhere in this section) and you can then choose how to respond.

However, there are times when you may want to state your position first in order to set expectations in the mind of the other party.

Before you even get to the marker stage, do your research; what does the market or independent benchmarks say about what's reasonable; establish the zone of acceptability and then start at the edge, or even outside of this.

If you need to lay down a marker, then aim high (seller) or low (buyer); make sure your position is stretching and realistic, as unrealistic demands make you look either out of touch or unreasonable.

If and when you do move from your original position, move reluctantly, slowly and modestly and avoid making a series of moves one after the other; if you've already moved several times, it implies you can and will move again.

LEAVING MONEY ON THE TABLE

This is a negotiation expression, derived from the game of poker, and which has been mentioned earlier, which means you could have made a better deal or achieved a better outcome. For example, asking for £70 per hour when the client, unknown to you, was more than happy to pay £90 per hour. Often, you will never know if you've left money on the table unless you push the other party to what you believe to be their limit.

It does not only relate to money, though. It could be any one of the other variables in the negotiation mix that you did not fully explain, expose, explore or exploit.

If you easily accept what the other party requests, then you're almost certainly leaving money on the table.

To avoid this, never say 'yes' to the first offer. Explore multiple variables, each of which has its own value, and get creative in devising a solution that means both parties come out with a deal where 2 + 2 really does equal 5 or more.

LEGACY CONTRACT

These are long-standing contracts or agreements that have run for many years, or even decades. They can be great win-win arrangements, involving strategic, long-term partnership agreements, but they can also tie an organisation down unnecessarily and prevent it from looking at new opportunities, alternatives and possibilities.

Contracts that have been rolling for several years can create inertia (see 'Switching Costs' elsewhere in this section). The original contracts can also become lost in the past, misplaced or they can morph over time, often in multiple variations, without the details of changes to the contract being formally documented or there being one, central, definitive agreement. It can be a nightmare for a new person joining an organisation and inheriting a legacy contract, whether as a supplier or buyer.

From a positive perspective, if you inherit a legacy contract, then that presents an opportunity to clarify and to continue the contract, but from a 'clean slate' of agreeing what it is exactly that has been agreed or has not. It might sound like an unnecessary piece of work, but it's one that might save a lot of trouble in the future.

LEVERAGE

See 'Nuisance'.

LIM: LIKE/INTEND/MUST

LIM is a negotiation tool for setting goals/targets.

L = what you would *like* to achieve in an ideal situation… the very best goal or target that you could achieve, though of course this still needs to be within the bounds of realism.

I = what you *intend* to achieve… the most realistic or likely outcome.

M = what you *must* achieve… your absolute minimum requirement.

However, as has been mentioned on multiple occasions in this book, it's not only about one variable, such as price. In any negotiation there are numerous variables that make up the 'negotiation mix'. In a commercial negotiation, in addition to price you might negotiate quantity, quality, delivery, phasing, payment terms, packaging, aftercare or additional services… to name just a few.

In preparation for a negotiation you need to brainstorm all the significant variables that are important in that situation, and then set LIM targets for *each* variable.

Step back and consider how these variables and targets are interdependent. Consider which you're prepared to move on, i.e. to be flexible in terms of bargaining, and which are non-negotiable. Consider which variables, if any, you're prepared to forego if you get what you want in other, more important variables – remember, it's about the 'whole deal'.

LOGICAL ARGUMENT

Convincing with logic is a powerful, legitimate influence and negotiation tool. It relies on objectivity, reason and rationale, and the fact that logical arguments are difficult to argue with.

It can include data, evidence, information, irrefutable facts and explanation of rationale.

Logic can also be used to counter seemingly irrational positions presented by the other party, undermining their argument and exposing its weakness, shortcomings, invalidity or fallibility.

You can use logic to counter logic – it's logical so difficult to argue with. If you're interested in reading further, the technique is called 'apply to self'.

LONG TERM VS. SHORT-TERM

People have different ideas as to how quickly things should happen in business. There are significant cultural aspects relating to the expectations of parties from different parts of the world. These mismatched expectations can create a sense of urgency or frustration on the side of one party, and a feeling of bewilderment or confusion on the other - which itself is something to be negotiated.

Another aspect is to consider the negotiation you're currently facing in the context of a longer timeline. Maybe a concession here and now, to clinch a short-term agreement, could be an investment in a future, bigger deal.

LOSS LEADER

A loss leader is a product or service which is offered to a consumer, or from one business to another, at a price that is either not profitable to the supplier, or even results in a financial net loss.

Why would any commercially minded company do this?

The reason is to get a toe-hold in the market, to attract new customers, to get those consumers hooked or to link it to the purchase of another product or service that is profitable to the supplier. For example, desktop printers are often sold at close to the cost price of manufacture because the company knows that consumers will then have to buy the (highly profitable) ink cartridges from them. It's the same with razors and razor blades. The profit on the latter is phenomenal and once you've bought the razor handle only that company's blades will fit it, so you're locked in.

In a business-to-business (B2B) environment, a supplier may agree to provide product A at cost price on the basis that the customer buys X quantity of product B. This is often referred to as a 'basket deal'.

M

MONOPOLIST

A monopolist supplier is the only supplier who is able to meet the needs of a particular customer.

Monopolists do not need to, but will often, exploit their position by keeping prices high, raising them above inflation, restricting supply or in general holding firm in negotiating because they know they're in a position of power.

There are several trade organisations that endeavour to ensure that monopolistic markets do not form, and they purport to be able to impose penalties on companies that pursue anti-competitive behaviour. Most are feeble and ineffective.

However, if you are a customer facing a monopolist, there are still things that you can do. Firstly, avoid getting into monopoly situations in the first place. If you do have a monopolistic supplier, don't beat yourself up over things that are largely out of your control. Join forces with the monopolist and try to work in partnership to jointly grow your business, getting them to reduce prices in return for higher volumes from your business. Work on personal relationships, so you're not just 'another purchase order'. Work hard to secure/maintain improved supplier performance so that at least you're not paying high prices for second-rate products or services.

Change your standards. Are you being too specific or fussy; could you get away with a different component or one that was not quite so highly specified?

Make it clear to them how unpleasant you find it doing business under these terms and in this atmosphere – appeal to reason and morals.

Make it clear that the current situation means you're examining other options. Search for alternative suppliers; perhaps they're small and just entering the market.

Search for suppliers of similar components or services; things that, with a bit of re-engineering of your market offering might be acceptable input substitutes.

Can you help one of your existing suppliers of a related product or service become an alternative supplier to the monopolist, an investment and 'win' for both of you?

Look for opportunities within the supplier's cost base to remove or reduce parts of their production and supply process, and hence reduce the cost to you.

Seek to remove parts of their product/service that are not so valuable to you. Ask for added-value services that are easy or cheap for the supplier to offer.

Finally, if supplier performance is unsatisfactory, seek an improvement plan against agreed objectives; poor performance is not acceptable, monopolist or not!

See also 'Oligopoly' and 'Cartel' elsewhere in this section.

N

NATURAL CONSEQUENCES

See 'Unintended Consequences'.

NEGOTIATION CRITERIA

Before you commence negotiation about the detail, consider negotiating with the other party to agree some criteria, principles or objective standards that you will then jointly apply to the substance of the negotiation itself. This is a different, but still highly relevant negotiation; it's about how we will negotiate; its about how we will decide.

Principled negotiators, using impartial, objective, third-party or other external reference points or benchmarks, create wise, fair agreements, amicably and efficiently. It's preferable to simply negotiating by brute willpower, emotion or unjustifiable stubbornness.

For example, when buying/selling a house, you could agree to take the value that a surveyor places on the property (or the average of three independent valuations). It's a benchmark from an uninvolved third party.

An objective assessment such as this is devoid of bias or personal interest, it's difficult to argue with and less vulnerable to attack. It also means that both parties can defer to a fair solution without feeling they've lost face or given in to the other. Most people respond to logic, data and reasoning.

NUISANCE

In negotiation parlance this is a term used by suppliers to describe the customers that they wish would go away! Not all suppliers are happy to supply certain customers if they make nuisances of themselves by being overly demanding, irksome, petty or where the value of the contract is frankly just not worth the effort.

In a supplier's market, nuisance customers get poor service or are even ignored. If the supplier does continue to serve the customer, then they'll typically do so in an exploitable manner, for example by raising prices way above inflation, in order to gain the maximum benefit from the relationship until the buyer ends it, typically.

In a buyer's market the buyer holds most, if not all of the power, and so they'll choose to leverage or squeeze the supplier. Why? Because they can easily go to another supplier at a moment's notice.

O

OBJECTIVE CRITERIA

See 'Negotiation Criteria'.

OLIGOPOLY

An oligopoly is a state of limited competition in which a market is shared by a small number of providers. They do not necessarily act in collusion, though some have been shown to do so, but as a small number of suppliers control supply and pricing, they effectively control the market and turn it into a seller's market. The products and services provided by oligopolistic companies are often largely similar, i.e. not particularly differentiated. Think of energy providers for example.

See also 'Monopolist' elsewhere in this section, for some ideas on how to deal with monopolistic or limited competition situations.

ONUS TRANSFER

Sometimes it's better to put the onus on to the other person/party to suggest what they think they should do, or should be done, in order to resolve a difficulty. Or, what it is that they want you to do if you're the one who's caused a problem.

This is similar to 'laying down a marker', mentioned elsewhere in this section. You're simply saying that there appears to be a problem, perhaps one that they've got themselves into, so what do they propose they should do about it?

In the latter case, if you're the apologising party, it may be the other party are not looking for significant compensation, and a simple, genuine apology from you is all they require.

When faced with a tricky situation where you're unsure whether to accept a problem, share it or transfer it to the other party, where you're deciding whether to state a price or to ask the other party what they were thinking of, consider asking them first.

What do they suggest as the next steps?

OPPORTUNITY COST

This is the cost of not doing what you could have done, having instead taken an alternative course of action.

When you're given several choices, only one of which is a realistic option, then there's a 'cost' of not choosing the others. This is not necessarily a bad thing, as often you cannot do everything or pursue multiple courses of action, and it would be folly to try.

A simple example is the loss of income that you could have achieved if you had left school and gone straight to work, rather than spending three or four years at university. However, one would hope that the lost income would be more than compensated by attaining a better paid job on graduation than would otherwise be the case. In the long term, the benefits, both financial and work-quality wise, are estimated to be worth the shorter-term opportunity cost.

P

PERSONAL AGENDAS

It's a fact of life that personal agendas – interests or positions that relate to what individuals want and need – and what's right for the business, get intertwined far more than is healthy or appropriate.

Everyone has personal agendas. The issue is the degree to which they let these affect their professional life and distort decisions they make, influence or implement. If you need evidence then look no further than the furore surrounding the awarding of locations for the football World Cup.

It can be costly and wasteful if personal interests are placed above the needs of the organisation, and with high value negotiations the stakes can be high.

Professional negotiators must put the interests of their organisation front of mind, not their own agenda. They must rise above the desire to attain a power base or advance a personal agenda, and direct conflict resolution towards creating and crafting the best possible solution for the entire organisation.

PERSONALISATION

When negotiations get personal and/or emotional, then a warning bell is sounding. They can escalate into personal attacks, accusations, insults or even just an exchange of sarcastic comments. The outcome is rarely good.

When emotions and egos become entangled in negotiations they adversely affects the ability of one party to see the other's position, interests and needs clearly. This results in adversarial rather than cooperative interactions.

Professional, principled negotiations make a clear distinction between jointly and rigorously tackling problems, and avoiding attacking the people involved. They clarify perceptions, put themselves in the shoes of the other party, they recognise when emotions are involved, communicate rationally and clearly, stick to the facts and try to remain objective.

POKER FACE

When playing poker, the last thing you want to do is to give away any information to the other players that might disadvantage your position. So, in negotiation parlance, playing with a poker face means not revealing your feelings about the situation or what has just been proposed.

The 'poker face' is a completely neutral facial expression that shows no emotion. It can come across as blank, cool, detached, reserved and unreadable. That's the point.

If you're presented with a fantastic deal, then perhaps it would be inadvisable to show your delight and gratitude by jumping up and down, smiling and immediately accepting.

That said, it can be draining and unenjoyable negotiating with people who show no emotion, excitement or energy. Like all things in life, it's about finding the right balance – in this case between showing enthusiasm for progressing the negotiation vs. not giving away too much.

A similar, game-based expression is 'keeping your cards close to your chest'.

POWER BALANCE

The power balance in a negotiation is incredibly important, and research shows that the degree of collaboration and cooperation between people in negotiations is related to where the 'balance of power' lies.

If the power balance is clearly on one side then they are clearly in a far stronger position, and they could exploit the imbalance against the other side.

There are numerous sources of power, which go to form this balance, including time, money, sanction, reward, reputation, networks, relationships, authority, information, access to limited resources, proprietary/branded goods and expertise, etc.

Good negotiators brainstorm all of the sources of power they have, they think broadly and creatively. They then brainstorm all of the sources of power they think the other party holds, and weigh the potency of all of the above to assess where the balance of power lies.

They then think of ways to increase the potency of their sources of power or, in the eyes of the other party, their 'perceived' strength/importance, and how they can reduce the potency of the sources of power of the other party.

PRECONDITIONING

Preconditioning between negotiating parties is about setting expectations in the mind(s) of the other before formal negotiations commence.

When does negotiation begin?

It's a lot sooner than you might think. Negotiation actually begins inside your head when you first become aware of a need or a want. You start to negotiate with yourself about how much you want or need a certain thing and how much you're prepared to pay for it. Or you negotiate with yourself about how much you're prepared to sell something for.

It can involve putting in high or low offers ahead of a discussion or meeting, stating what is and what is not going to be on the negotiation table or ring-fencing issues as in, *'I'm happy to meet, but please understand that if you want to talk about price increases this year, you're wasting your time – sorry',* or referring to big uncomfortable factors such as company-wide cost cutting, redundancies, reducing the number of suppliers, etc.

Other examples include highlighting credentials, reputation, company size and references, etc. – indicating to a purchaser that your services are in high demand and you already have an almost full schedule or order book so they need to act fast.

More aggressive tactics include not answering calls or emails, keeping visitors waiting in reception, adopting an unfriendly attitude or not offering refreshments etc. The author recommends none of these crass, asinine, blunt and foolish tactics.

Retain an awareness of how and where you might be on the receiving end of preconditioning and refuse to be manipulated psychologically.

R

RAPPORT

Rapport is a critical life skill. When you're in rapport with someone you 'click', you get along with another person and you achieve things in an effortless way. Partly it's natural chemistry; though you can consciously develop rapport with others. Just a few techniques include:

- Taking a genuine interest in, and getting to know what's important to the other person, seeing the world through their eyes, trying to understand them rather than expecting them to understand you first.

- Subtly matching and mirroring some of their behaviours: voice tonality, speed of speaking, breathing rate, the rhythm of their movement, body postures, gestures and their general energy level.

- Noticing how they like to handle information: lots of detail or just the big picture? Are they more visual, auditory or kinaesthetic? As you communicate, feed back information in a way that is most likely to resonate with them. Notice the key words, expressions and favourite phrases that a person uses and then subtly build some of these into your own conversation. Avoid using the terms 'I' and 'you'; instead use collective terms like 'we' and 'us'. This simple switch of language alone can be hugely powerful.

RECESS

Seeking an adjournment to consolidate, review, recalculate or possibly reshape a deal can be a good tactic. New ideas often emerge if a break is taken, away from the stress of the live negotiation. It often encourages one or both parties to reconsider their stance and the reasonableness of the positions they have taken. It also enables each party to consult with their internal stakeholders, which may bring greater flexibility back to the table.

Recesses are also helpful when emotions are running high, or when you're negotiating as a team and things are beginning to fall apart. A recess can result in a renewal of energy and concentration; it can also help to break a deadlock.

See 'Deadlock' and 'Emotion' elsewhere in this section.

RECIPROCITY

Most people feel an overwhelming urge to repay debts, to do something in return when something is done for them, a favour, a kindness, or an unexpected gift. You know this is right; you feel it yourself.

Psychologists and sociologists assert that the urge to reciprocate is a universal principle that transcends cultures. It means that we're all bound, even driven, to repay debts of many kinds. When someone has done something meaningful for us in the past, and they ask for a favour later, we often quickly and automatically say 'Yes', because subconsciously we know we're indebted to them, and we need the psychological release to be able to feel that the 'books are balanced'.

See '27 Reciprocity' case for more detail.

RED HERRING

The term 'red herring' originates in the use of a strong-smelling kipper to train hounds to follow a scent when hunting, or to divert them off the trail.

In negotiation terms, it's about pretending you want something else in order to get what you really want. A buyer may focus attention on a minor issue in order to get her way on a major one. For example, she might suggest that her reason for not being able to agree to 'X' is because of 'Y'. She gives in to X later, on the condition that you provide 'Z'. The point is that 'Y' was never an issue for her in the first place; it was a 'red herring'.

See '49 Red Herring' case for more detail.

RISK SHARING

Also known as 'risk distribution', this simply means that both parties take a share in both the benefits of a deal working out, and the risks (often costs) if it does not.

Risk sharing can be a useful approach when the future is particularly uncertain. So, a supplier may agree to provide a product to a business customer, who is then going to market that product to the general public. However, until they launch the product there are no guarantees about how many will ultimately be sold. So, the supplier may agree to supply at a certain price without having any guarantees about volume, and the intermediary absorbs all of the sales and marketing costs, again, without any guarantees that these costs will be repaid with profits from sales.

RUSSIAN FRONT

As described in the case with the same name, the 'Russian front' tactic describes a situation in which one party presents the other with just two options. One is so awful (like being sent to fight on the cold and frozen Russian front) that they agree to the alternative, as it's the least-worst option.

The Russian Front option may not be completely awful, but it is almost certainly one the other party will not choose. Two options are being presented, but in effect there is only one that is acceptable. Offering something that is clearly undesirable creates panic and discomfort, something that the other party will want to move away from.

See case 52 – 'Russian Front' for more detail.

S

SANCTION

Sanction has an interesting double meaning in English. It can either mean a threatened penalty to be imposed, i.e. something negative, or it can mean granting official permission or approval for what is proposed, i.e. something positive.

In negotiations you can use the threat of a negative sanction, a penalty, in order to influence the future decisions and/or behaviour of the other party. An example would be the imposition of financial penalties for late delivery. This is the 'stick' approach of carrot and stick.

You can also use the 'carrot' of offering an incentive for the other party to agree to a certain deal or condition. An example would be: *'If you're able to guarantee delivery by 25th of the month, then I'm prepared to sign (sanction) the contract today.'*

SAVING FACE

Saving face, or one's pride or reputation, can be a strong personal driver in a negotiation, yet it's often hidden. One party may have continued to hold out on an issue, or they realise they've made a mistake, and now feel they need to back track, but to do so would be to admit defeat or some form of weakness on their part.

People negotiate on both business and personal levels. If one party suffers loss of face in dealing with another, even the best agreement will leave a bitter aftertaste. All of us need to validate our self-worth. When our self-image is threatened, hostility emerges, which manifests itself in anger and perhaps retribution, even if taking such a reprisal damages their position. The 12th-century English expression 'to cut your nose off to spite your face' is used to describe a needlessly self-destructive over-reaction to a problem.

If you suspect a person is looking to save face, then there are things you can do to help them. You can try blaming people outside of the situation who have since left or are no longer involved. You can point to things that are in neither your nor their control. You can state that you can see their perspective, but maybe you've not fully or clearly explained the situation, and you then rephrase or re-frame the situation. You can present some 'new' information or factors to consider and, as the situation is then changed, this gives them an opportunity to say something like, *'Okay, when you present it like that I can see your point – perhaps I can reconsider.'*

SCARCITY

Fear of loss is a powerful motivator, as is the fear of losing out on a possible gain. By leveraging the instinctive human tendency to avoid losing what one already possesses, or avoid losing out on the chance to possess something desirable, you can trigger a psychological and, therefore, behavioural response.

See '3 Scarcity' case for more detail.

STAKEHOLDERS

A stakeholder is any person who has an interest in the outcome of the negotiation. They may want it to succeed, or they may want it to fail. Don't assume that all stakeholders are looking for the achievement of a successful negotiated outcome.

When multiple stakeholders are involved, then a negotiation can become an even more complex and, at times, tricky game.

Stakeholders can be both internal and external. A purchaser may have multiple internal stakeholders to satisfy and so the negotiation with them can sometimes be more problematic than that with a supplier.

STRATEGIC PARTNERSHIP

How many strategic partners can you have?

Very few - maybe only one.

Strategic partnerships tend to be long term, mutually interdependent, high value and crucial/core to both parties' interests or situation.

These are in contrast with transactional relationships, which are one-off and short term. Whilst the value of the latter can be low or high, they tend to be single transactions and neither party has much, if any, interest in continuing a relationship after conclusion of the deal. One of the advantages of a transactional negotiation is that you do not expect to see the other party again (unless there's a problem).

Another difference between strategic and transactional negotiations is that in the latter you can use some of the harder negotiation tactics to try to get the very best deal you can, quite simply because it's a one-off deal and you don't need to preserve a relationship afterwards.

SUNK COST

Sunk costs occur when a person has invested time, money, personal energy, passion or other resources into a project – resources that can't be recovered.

People naturally don't want to have wasted past investments and, therefore, they tend to include them as relevant information in deciding how to move forwards.

Imagine you've invested time and money in designing a new e-system but, despite several attempts, it's just not working. The costs of throwing it out and starting again will be a factor in any decision about how to proceed, but including sunk costs introduces a bias towards staying with the status quo, even when the decision to do so is not the best.

You may be better served by starting again, even though it galls you to do so. The investment has already been lost, and so it is no longer relevant to present or future decisions.

In negotiations, whenever practical, the person who was most personally invested in a previous decision should take a step back. They need to remind themselves of their inclination, preferences and personal involvement and, therefore, to take that into account throughout the future decision-making process.

SWITCHING COSTS

These are the negative costs incurred as a result of changing suppliers, brands or products.

Although they're mostly defined in monetary terms, there are also psychological, effort and time-based costs involved in making a change. If you have been with a particular provider for many years, there are a lot of things that you will potentially 'throw away' if you change to another supplier.

Suppliers often try to tie in customers by making it hard for them to change or switch suppliers – for example by imposing cancellation charges or by making the process to change overly complicated and time consuming.

Suppliers will also rely upon inertia – the 'can't be bothered to change or even look at other options' attitude from customers that plagues many people in a time poor environment.

If the cost to change is small and the benefits great, then of course you will switch. If you don't want the hassle, the risk is too high or the benefits neither substantial nor guaranteed, then you probably won't.

T

THIRD-PARTY BENCHMARK

See 'Negotiation Criteria'.

THREAT

The use of threat, or 'implied threat', is a legitimate negotiation tactic. However, like anything with immense force, such as a hammer, it needs to be handled carefully and... you can damage yourself in the process! Threat can have both intended and unintended consequences; so be careful.

For a threat to have legitimacy, and for you to have credibility in wielding it, you need to be prepared to follow through with action; otherwise do not threaten.

See case 9 – 'Using Threat' for more information.

TIME VALUE OF MONEY

In essence, this means that money available now is worth more than money available, or promised to be available, in the future.

Money now enables you to do things with it, to leverage it, invest, or to meet the needs of short-term cash flow. Money in the future is of no use if you're going bust next week!

If interest rates are positive, then you can earn interest on money now, but £100 in the future, at an interest rate of 5%, means you only receive the equivalent today of £95.24 in one year's time.

TRANSACTION

See 'Strategic Partnership'.

U

UNINTENDED CONSEQUENCES

Unintended consequences are outcomes that were not foreseen or intended by an action or decision taken in a negotiation. They can be both positive and negative.

Unintended consequences can arise simply because the situation is so complex that the various parties cannot think of everything. It could be because the logical natural consequences were simply not thought about, or because something occurs as a result of an action that could not have been anticipated. The development of Aspirin as a pain reliever was later discovered to have beneficial anti-coagulant properties, which can prevent heart attacks – something that could not have been predicted before the drug was launched. Viagra was originally developed to combat hypertension. It did not, as the original researchers had hoped, reduce blood pressure. But it did produce erections in 80% of men to whom it was prescribed.

In negotiations it is often useful to take time out to think through the 'natural' (most likely or possible) consequences of a certain action, before taking it or proposing it. If you run the 'video' in your head, it can help you to possibly not make that decision, or to put caveats around it to minimise the risk of doing so. Prevention is better than cure.

You can also use the natural consequences tactic to get the other party to think through the scenario in their own mind, creating their own mental video of the likely natural consequences of whatever they're proposing – either positive or negative. When they create and run their own mental video, it will be far more powerful than anything you can tell them.

See also 'Threat' elsewhere in this section.

URGENCY

See 'Desperation', 'Deadlines' and 'Long Term vs. Short-Term' elsewhere in this section.

V

VALUE VS. PRICE

Price is not the same as value. Price is an objective number, the ticket price or the price you actually pay for something. Value is far more subjective, and usually more important. The value of a product or service can vary wildly between those perceiving it and the situation they're in. If you're desperate to have something, you're likely to pay any price because the 'value' of the item or service is far more important than its price.

Also, people don't buy on price alone; in fact, sometimes price is not the most important factor. Many variables are involved, and in negotiation it's critical to find out which variables are most important (valuable) to the other party. Is it quality, reliability, flexibility, speed of availability, prestige, ego or something else?

Some things can be too cheap, and a common negotiation expression is: *'If you buy cheap, you end up buying twice.'*

Moral – don't be a cheapskate!

VARIABLES

Beware of assuming that any particular negotiation is confined to just one or two issues, such as price or quantity. It's common for a negotiation to involve multiple variables, in some cases more than 40.

If you focus on just one aspect, such as price, then this can become all consuming; you may find you get stuck and deadlock ensues.

Negotiation is made possible because of the 'magic' of variables, each of which has a value, and each of which can be flexed and traded in order to reach an overall negotiated agreement.

Write down the variables for a particular negotiation; this forces you to think about even more variables – the ones you have not yet considered. Keep all of these in mind all of the time. Keep searching for variables as things change, new information comes to light, and you jointly search for alternative ways of configuring the deal. Remain flexible and open to ideas and suggestions; do not wear your plan like a straitjacket. Know your limits, how far you can move on each variable, your LIM (see 'LIM' elsewhere in this section), what you would need in return if you were to move and your BATNA (Best Alternative To a Negotiated Agreement). Know the interests of the other party, the variables that are the most important to them, why they're important and the value each variables has for them.

WALK AWAY

One of the most powerful tactics you can use in a negotiation is to threaten to walk away from the table. You don't actually have to walk away, you simply imply that you're getting close to it or that you will walk away if necessary.

However, it's a dangerous game to play unless you have a BATNA (Best Alternative To a Negotiated Agreement). If the other party calls your bluff and you do not have a BATNA, or you're not genuinely prepared to walk away, then you may quickly find yourself in a lose-lose situation.

See case 20 – 'BATNA and Walk Away Power' for more information.

WIDOWS AND ORPHANS

See 'Guilt' elsewhere in this section.

WIN-WIN

The philosophy of 'win-win' negotiating is that 2 + 2 can equal 5, 50 or 507.

Stephen Covey describes win-win thinking as a frame of mind that constantly seeks mutual benefit in all human interactions – agreements or solutions that are satisfying to all involved. It's not idealistic nonsense; it can be achieved and often is.

Sadly, some people think in terms of competitive dichotomies: strong or weak, win or lose, tough or nice. But win-win thinking centres on the paradigm that there is plenty for everybody, and that one person's success is not achieved at the expense or exclusion of another person. If we get creative, we can all win in our own way; we don't divide the pie… we work together to make the pie bigger!

It's just a shame that Simon Goh Chan from case 23 did not think of that!

Win-win is tough and nice, courageous and empathetic, brave and sensitive. To do this, to achieve a balance between courage and consideration, is the essence of real maturity in negotiating, in business and in life in general.

See also 'Zero-Sum Game', next in this section.

Z

ZERO-SUM GAME

So, continuing from the previous paragraph, if you only have, or see, one 'pie' and you take more than 50%, it means the other person gets less. This is called playing a 'zero-sum game', also known as 'distributive bargaining'.

It's crude and unimaginative. It assumes that my win is your loss and vice versa. It also assumes that there are no other variables involved, and it precludes the chance to be imaginative and to create multiple options between us.

The approach of creating multiple options is not about dividing a single pie – it's about making the pie bigger.

So, start with the assumption that there's a variable amount and range of different resources to be divided, and both sides can 'win' in their unique way. The goal is for you to maximise joint outcomes, using cooperation, information sharing and mutual problem solving. This approach creates value since both parties leave the negotiation feeling they've achieved greater value for themselves than before. Together, value has been created that did not exist before.

This is not idealistic nonsense, it really can be and has been done.

ZOPA

ZOPA refers to the 'Zone of Potential Agreement' that exists between two negotiating parties.

If no ZOPA exists, then it is unlikely, though not impossible, that an agreement can be made.

As you will have read in case 46 – 'ZOPA', the example below is given.

Imagine, for example, that the only variable is price; the seller is not willing to sell for less than €10,000 and the buyer is not willing to pay more than €9,000, then a deal does not appear to be possible; a state of 'stalemate' exists. However, if the seller's privately known minimum price is €9,000 and the seller is secretly prepared to go as high as €9,500, then a deal is possible.

However, and as has been discussed many times in this book, in most negotiations there are far more variables involved, and so a deal may be possible where no ZOPA appears to exist for one particular variable. For example, the seller may be prepared to accept less money if the buyer were to buy in cash on the spot, or allow the seller to remove an aspect of the product or reconfigure the service. The buyer may be prepared to pay more if the seller were to offer free delivery, allow staged payments over a six-month period or provide an extended warranty, etc.

Successful negotiators deal with multiple variables simultaneously and make trades between them. It can take time, but it's worth it. The eventual deal results in an effective configuration of agreements within ZOPAs for multiple variables.

FINAL THOUGHTS...

Dear negotiator,

I hope this was an interesting and insightful journey for you, vicariously walking through the experiences of 52 other people.

It has certainly been inspiring for me to bring these cases together, and to extract from them some valuable insights and lessons.

The journey continues of course; it does not end here – but this book does need to end somewhere! So, to conclude, I want to leave you with four final thoughts, and a call to action in the 'postscript'.

1 PRACTISE IN SMALL WAYS

What do I mean by this? It sounds rather unambitious.

Each of the cases you've read had consequences – good or bad, helpful or horrible, surprising or reassuring.

When you're faced with a really important negotiation, the outcome of which could have a tremendous impact on you, positively or negatively, then of course you need to be as good as you can possibly be. You not only need to know how best to conduct yourself in terms of negotiation strategy and tactics, but you also need to be practised in doing so. Practice makes you close to perfect.

So, for example, in case 7 - 'The Power of Silence' the consequences of getting it wrong were minimal. Such simple situations present ideal opportunities for you to try out your skills, develop new skills, refine your technique, observe what happens, reflect on this and learn from the experience.

When you're later faced with a much more significant negotiation, perhaps discussing a big business deal or the sale of your house, then using exactly the same technique may yield 10, 100 or even 1000 times the benefit in tangible terms. The fact that you've practised it in a number of previous, relatively small ways means you have a degree of experience, and greater confidence in using the technique in this far more important situation when the stakes are higher.

2 REGARD EVERY SITUATION AS AN OPPORTUNITY TO NEGOTIATE

Okay, perhaps you should not negotiate in *every* situation, but I did not mean that. I mean regard every situation as an *opportunity* to negotiate.

Sometimes it's best just to go with the flow, relax a little and focus on the bigger picture, the longer-term game or ultimate objective.

If you turn every interaction with another person into a negotiation, then it can become tiring and make for a difficult journey through life. If you respond to your wife/husband who says, *'Can we watch my favourite film tonight?'* with *'Maybe, but only if you give me a back scratch first'*, you're probably heading for the divorce courts, and that's a whole different negotiation you don't want to find yourself in!

However, there are some people who let things go too soon or too easily. They put up with shoddy service in a restaurant, a steak that's not cooked exactly to their liking, a wine that seems to smell a bit 'funny' but they swallow it, don't say anything, and spend half the night in the bathroom. Or, in a commercial deal, they accept the first price they're offered without even thinking that almost everything is negotiable – even government taxes, if they push back strongly enough. Even the debt restructuring of entire countries!

As long as you're not damaging the relationship, hurting someone else or damaging your health by getting angry, frustrated, stressed and losing control, then look for those moments in your day when a negotiation is possible, and you have a little time to experiment – and have some fun in the process!

3 IT WON'T ALWAYS WORK

Don't beat yourself up when your attempts to negotiate a better outcome, a sweeter deal or to resolve an issue to your full satisfaction don't work out as you had originally hoped.

At the time of writing this final section of the book I had an issue at a hotel I was staying in with my wife. It's marketed as a high-class, 'get away from it all' relaxing beach hotel. It cost a lot of money and, if you recall from case 17 - 'Good, Cheap, Fast', then you will understand that I was expecting the whole experience to be *'reassuringly* expensive'!

After three days of relaxing... a party of, what I would politely describe as, 'overly enthusiastic, unnecessarily loud and gregarious people' arrived. There were 10 of them, five guys and five girls, all in their early thirties, clearly determined to have a great time, possibly at the expense of everyone else.

I tolerated this for most of the day, even though it significantly prevented us from enjoying our 'relaxing' holiday. But the tipping point for me was when I later walked past the pool to see the five guys all standing in the water drinking beer from glass bottles.

Rather than confront them directly – which might have been an unwise move considering there were five of them, I was only dressed in my swim shorts, they were well-built and each was 'armed' with a glass bottle – I went and spoke immediately to the hotel manager. I expressed my utter disbelief that the hotel staff would allow people to be in the swimming pool (kids and families were around) with glass bottles.

My appeal was met with swift action, and within five minutes the guys were sitting away from the pool, drinking their beer from what are oxymoronically described as 'plastic glasses'.

The hotel manager apologised and asked if there was anything he could do to make up for the inconvenience and upset. I said I did not know, but would think about it. He then said, *'How about if we give you and your wife dinner with our compliments some time during the rest of your stay with us?'* I thanked him for the offer and said that, again, I wanted to think about it as we were staying for another six days.

The next day the rowdiness continued, though the pool incident did not. Having tolerated this now for two days, I went to see the hotel manager again and said that I had thought about his offer, but two nights' free accommodation would be more acceptable to compensate us for the last two days of disturbance to our holiday and that, due to the heat (we were in a tropical location), we had both lost our appetites and had not been in the mood for a big dinner on previous nights.

To cut a long story short, getting two nights' accommodation knocked off our bill was not going to happen, but the free dinner was still on offer if we chose to accept it. The following day, having spent a few hours still disgruntled at not managing to achieve my objective, I gratefully accepted the free dinner.

That afternoon the 10 guests departed.

That evening we had a great time and a free dinner – our appetites had returned.

The lesson for me is that negotiation will not always work, but sometimes you need to step back and ask yourself if you're being too ambitious or, in my case, perhaps greedy in what you ask for.

Also, don't set yourself targets so high that you're unlikely to meet, and then beat yourself up unnecessarily as a consequence.

This negotiation did yield a positive outcome, just not the one I had set my sights on. That said, there was a nice touch at the end as the hotel manager came over to us as we were getting into the taxi to the airport to say, *'Sir/Madam, it's been a pleasure having you stay with us this week. Don't worry about paying for the taxi, we're putting it on our account – have a safe flight home.'*

4 LIGHTEN UP AND ENJOY THE GAME

As mentioned in the Introduction, negotiation is a game, and games are to be enjoyed.

To paraphrase the lady mountaineer Yvon Chouinard...

> *'How you climb a mountain is as important as reaching the top.'*

Good luck on your journey to new heights!

Jon

POSTSCRIPT

Like you, I am a voracious learner, and in my role as an international negotiation skills trainer/facilitator and author, I look for every opportunity to share interesting stories and good ideas wherever possible, to all who are equally keen to learn.

As you picked up this book and read it to the end, then you clearly have an interest in, and experience of, negotiations yourself.

If you would like to share a brief summary of a negotiation or two that sticks in your mind, and for which an insight or lesson can be drawn, then I would love to hear from you, particularly if your example is unusual or interesting in some way. Take your lead from the examples included in this book. Don't worry about having to write it all out in detail. Sometimes all I need is a brief paragraph and I can then draw out the insights and lessons, etc.

If I include your example in a future edition of this book, then with your permission I will credit you in the introductory section and ensure you get to approve the final version of the case before publication. I will also send you a free, signed copy of the book when published.

You can send any suggestions to me at
jon@managertoolkits.co.uk or jon@blueiceconsulting.co.uk

Together we learn more…

together we grow…

together we're stronger…

together we succeed.

PERSONAL NOTES

PERSONAL NOTES

PERSONAL NOTES

PERSONAL NOTES

PERSONAL NOTES

PERSONAL NOTES

Manager Toolkits Ltd
www.managertoolkits.co.uk

In today's time-poor environment you're probably looking for quick, effective pragmatic solutions. Maybe you don't have time to attend training courses, do comprehensive research, explore theories of management or read lots of books.

Manager Toolkits designs, and prints handy A6 sized personal productivity, management, strategic and negotiation skills toolkits that can save you hundreds of hours of research, reading and unproductive effort. Currently we have five toolkits available. Just one of these is profiled below – the 'Advanced Negotiator's Toolkit'.

Each toolkit contains only the very best practical advice about what works in the real world of work - all the waffle and twaddle is cut out!

Visit www.managertoolkits.co.uk to find out more and view free samples.

| Introduction to Negotiation | Information and Planning | Engaging and Communicating | Influencing and Negotiating | Deal Making | Resolving Difficulties | Manager Toolkits Ltd |

Advanced Negotiator's Toolkit
Effective business negotiation strategies, tools and tactics

1 Introduction to Negotiation
- Win-Win Negotiating
- Negotiation Process
- Reason and Reasonableness
- Price vs. Value
- Interests vs. Positions
- People vs. Problems
- Creating Multiple Options
- Using Impartial Benchmarks
- Negotiating as a Team

2 Information and Planning
- TOWS (SWOT) Analysis
- Porter's Five Forces
- Setting LIM Targets
- BATNA
- ZOPA
- Exploring Variables
- Sources of Power
- Stakeholder Analysis
- Stakeholder Mapping
- Planning for the Meeting

3 Engaging and Communicating
- Psychology of Room Layout
- Building Rapport
- Personality Styles
- Flexing Personal Styles
- Developing Trust
- Power of Questions
- Types of Questions
- Active Listening Behaviours
- Power Listening
- Communication Preferences

4 Influencing and Negotiating
- Convincing With Logic
- Using Emotion
- Using Threat
- Spotting Liars Non-Verbally
- Spotting Liars Verbally
- Reciprocity
- Commitment and Consistency
- Similarity and Liking
- Authority
- Social Proof
- Scarcity

5 Deal Making
- Handling Personal Agendas
- Perceptual Positions
- Using Perceptual Positions
- Juggling Variables
- Magic of Movement
- Importance of Time
- Bargaining
- Trading Concessions
- Hypothesising
- Compromising

6 Resolving Difficulties
- Dealing with Big Egos
- Responses to Conflict
- Resolving Differences
- Dealing with Deadlock
- Dealing with Monopolists
- Cultural Iceberg Model
- Cultural Awareness
- Cultural Dimensions
- Emotional Intelligence
- Negotiating with Psychopaths

www.managertoolkits.co.uk

"One of the best personal development books we've come across for some time."
David Bowman: Anglo-American Books

"If you need a helping hand on how to survive in this life… this is the book."
David Birch: Professional coach and counsellor

"Brilliant; inspiring, practical and made me laugh!"
Koen Jansen: Business Development Manager

"Techniques that really work!"
Richard Summerfield: HR Director

"The psychological equivalent of an end of day double Gin & Tonic – this book is a life-changer."
Paul McGee: Keynote Speaker

Learn How To...

- Win in more arguments
- Deal with workplace bullies, irritating, awkward and exasperating people
- Deal effectively with 'unreasonable' people and counter their demands in a professional manner
- Take greater control over how you think about situations and events - explore psychological strategies and secrets known only by a tiny minority
- Respond to people and circumstances in ways that leave you laughing with tears, not crying!
- Spot people who manipulate, use verbal tricks or play 'mind games',

and respond professionally and potently to neutralise or reverse their impact

- Deal decisively with people who exaggerate, make unfair judgements or dubious connections, distort facts, spread rumours, or twist things to suit their own ends
- Build strong, unshakeable confidence in your ability to deal with anything that people and life throw at you
- Develop mental mastery and peak psychological fitness
- Be happier – knowing you're in control